# Alan Turing

## Breaking Boundaries in Science and Technology

*(His Research of Cybernetics, Morphogenesis, Artificial Intelligence and Neural Networks)*

**Alfred Vasquez**

Published By **Windy Dawson**

# Alfred Vasquez

*Alan Turing: Breaking Boundaries in Science and Technology (His Research of Cybernetics, Morphogenesis, Artificial Intelligence and Neural Networks)*

**ISBN 978-1-7781462-5-1**

No part of this guidebook shall be reproduced in any form without permission in writing from the publisher except in the case of brief quotations embodied in critical articles or reviews.

Legal & Disclaimer

The information contained in this book is not designed to replace or take the place of any form of medicine or professional medical advice. The information in this book has been provided for educational & entertainment purposes only.

The information contained in this book has been compiled from sources deemed reliable, and it is accurate to the best of the Author's knowledge; however, the Author cannot guarantee its accuracy and validity and cannot be held liable for any errors or omissions. Changes are periodically made to this book. You must consult your doctor or get professional medical advice before using any of the suggested remedies, techniques, or information in this book.

# Table Of Contents

Chapter 1: Early Life and Upbringing ........1

Chapter 2: The Emergence of a Mathematician..........................................7

Chapter 3: Personal Life and Challenges.18

Chapter 4: Artificial Intelligence Pioneer 28

Chapter 5: Impact on Mathematics ........41

Chapter 6: The Global Impact of Alan Turing .....................................................56

Chapter 7: Alan Turing's Childhood.........69

Chapter 8: The Early Signs of Intellect ....78

Chapter 9: Turing's Contribution to Mathematical Logic.................................84

Chapter 10: The Arrival at Bletchley Park92

Chapter 11: Deciphering the Indecipherable ......................................102

Chapter 12: The Turing Machine...........109

Chapter 13: A Secret Wedding..............115

Chapter 14: The Turing Trial..................120

Chapter 15: The Dramatic Epilogue ......125

Chapter 16: Legacy and Credits............131

Chapter 17: Child Prodigy ....................136

Chapter 18: Turing Machine .................147

Chapter 19: Post-War Years and Artificial Intelligence...........................................158

Chapter 20: The Enigma of Alan Turing 168

Chapter 21: Quotes and Sayings ..........180

# Chapter 1: Early Life and Upbringing

Childhood in Maida Vale

Alan Mathison Turing, the high-quality mind whose contributions to technological know-how and generation may end up legendary, started out out his existence's journey inside the quiet suburban network of Maida Vale, London. Born on June 23, 1912, more youthful Alan became the second of sons to Julius Mathison Turing and Ethel Sara Stoney. His upbringing, whilst marked via manner of privilege, changed into not without its specific demanding conditions.

Family Background and Influences

Alan's father, Julius, become a high-quality member of the Indian Civil Service, retaining the location of District Officer within the Indian Civil Service. The family's connections to India exposed Alan to a international of severa cultures and thoughts that would go away an indelible mark on his worldview.

Ethel Sara Stoney, Alan's mom, modified into the daughter of Edward Waller Stoney, the chief engineer of the Madras Railways. Her lineage have grow to be steeped in the sciences and engineering, and she or he or he or he had a particular ardour for botany. Alan's maternal grandfather's have an impact on on his mother's interests may additionally want to later be contemplated in Alan's very very own inclination within the route of the logical and systematic.

From an early age, Alan have become uncovered to a wealthy highbrow surroundings. The Turing circle of relatives changed into full of books on a big range of subjects, nurturing his innate interest. Young Alan might spend hours immersed inside the international of literature, technological know-how, and puzzles, developing a precocious mind.

Early Demonstrations of Genius

As Alan grew, it have turn out to be clean that his thoughts have become remarkable. At St.

Michael's, an afternoon school in St. Leonards-on-Sea, he displayed an early affinity for arithmetic and technological knowledge. It became at some stage in this time that the seeds of his love for common enjoy and hassle-solving had been sown. While his education furnished a strong foundation, it modified into the spark of interest and creativity that set him apart.

In his early years, Alan's pursuits had been eclectic. He had a penchant for nature, and he explored the geographical region, collecting specimens and displaying a deep fascination with the area's complicated workings. This natural hobby may want to later growth to his mathematical pursuits.

The basis for Alan Turing's highbrow journey were laid in the ones childhood. He became a little one of privilege, blessed with get right of entry to to information, a supportive own family, and the surroundings that nurtured his burgeoning genius. Yet, it turn out to be the suitable mixture of those factors, alongside

3

together together together with his innate brilliance, that set the extent for a remarkable lifestyles dedicated to breaking barriers in technological understanding and era.

Join me as we delve deeper into the life of Alan Turing, exploring the impacts that traditional his individual and mind, and the exceptional journey that would see him emerge as a pioneer within the fields of arithmetic, commonplace sense, laptop era, codebreaking, and artificial intelligence. Alan Turing have become destined for greatness, and his formative years supplied the fertile ground from which his legacy may want to grow.

Education and Academic Prowess

Schooling and Early Interest in Mathematics

Alan Turing's journey from a precocious infant to a groundbreaking mathematician and philosopher grow to be marked by way of manner of way of educational milestones that might lay the muse for his destiny achievements. His early interest in mathematics, nurtured via his family and his time at St. Michael's college in St. Leonards-on-Sea, end up the primary glimpse of his superb potential.

At St. Michael's, Turing's fascination with arithmetic have come to be increasingly more obtrusive. He showed a tremendous flair for solving complicated mathematical puzzles and set up a degree of hobby that set him aside from his pals. These early reviews kindled his love for numbers and commonplace feel, which could end up precious to his lifestyles's work.

Admission to King's College, Cambridge

Turing's outstanding mathematical abilities did now not skip disregarded. In 1926, on the age of 14, he released into the subsequent segment of his educational journey through the usage of enrolling at Sherborne School, an all-boys boarding college in Dorset. It changed into at Sherborne that he persevered to excel academically, but it changed into moreover wherein he confronted the demanding conditions of conforming to the traditional academic machine. His precise thoughts set him apart, and he observed camaraderie with a small circle of like-minded buddies who shared his ardour for era and mathematics.

Upon completing his training at Sherborne, Turing endured to Cambridge, one of the international's important facilities of reading. He joined King's College, Cambridge, in 1931, wherein he studied arithmetic under the steerage of the famend mathematician Max Newman. It changed into sooner or later of this period that Turing's intellectual contributions started out to take shape.

# Chapter 2: The Emergence of a Mathematician

Turing's Significant Mathematical Contributions

The early Nineteen Thirties marked a pivotal duration in Alan Turing's lifestyles. Armed with a top notch mind and an insatiable hobby, he delved into the area of mathematics and good judgment, embarking on a adventure that would all of the time adjust the landscape of these disciplines.

During this time, Turing was introduced to foundational questions in mathematics, mainly the idea of decidability. His insights into those inquiries may want to lay the groundwork for groundbreaking contributions that could resonate via the corridors of academia for decades to come lower again.

At the coronary coronary heart of Turing's highbrow adventure became the improvement of the concept of computability. He sought to address the question of what it meant for a mathematical problem to be "computable." In reaction to this venture, he brought the belief of a "common gadget" or a theoretical bring together capable of performing any mathematical computation that is probably defined thru an set of regulations.

This concept, which may additionally later end up known as the Turing machine, have become modern-day. It represented a shift a long way from the constraints of bodily device and centered on abstract strategies of computation. The Turing gadget served as a theoretical version that transcended the limitations of any specific bodily computer and spread out new vistas within the realm of arithmetic and pc technological knowledge.

The Decision Problem and its Significance

As Turing endured to discover the guidelines of arithmetic, he have emerge as deeply engrossed inside the "choice hassle," a query posed with the aid of manner of mathematician David Hilbert. The choice trouble sought to determine whether there existed a normal set of policies or system capable of figuring out the reality or falsity of any mathematical announcement.

Turing's art work in this hassle become groundbreaking. In collaboration with Alonzo Church, he showed that no such tremendous choice system may additionally moreover want to exist, successfully resolving a long-popularity query within the global of mathematical commonplace experience. This revelation, referred to as the Church-Turing thesis, have come to be a cornerstone of the idea of computation and laid the muse for the emergence of pc technology as a remarkable subject.

Shaping the Landscape of Modern Mathematics

Alan Turing's contributions in this era marked a turning aspect within the records of mathematics. His work on computability and the selection trouble provided a theoretical framework that underpinned the development of the modern-day laptop and the technological understanding of computation. The Turing system, a concept born of his tremendous thoughts, have become the blueprint for the digital laptop systems that could emerge many years later.

Turing's artwork now not best revolutionized the theoretical panorama of mathematics but furthermore had profound implications for the development of computer science, synthetic intelligence, and information concept. His mind became the theoretical underpinning for the digital age, shaping the technology and improvements that outline the twenty first century.

In the chapters that follow, we will delve deeper into the outstanding existence and contributions of Alan Turing. We will discover how his mind extended past theoretical constructs, vital to realistic innovations that for all time changed the area of technological understanding and era. Turing changed into not merely a mathematician; he end up a trailblazer who opened doors to new geographical regions of human information and technological improvement.

## Turing's Machines: The Birth of Computer Science

### Conceptualizing the Turing Machine

Alan Turing's adventure into the heart of computer technological know-how reached its zenith with the concept of the Turing tool, a theoretical gather that would grow to be a cornerstone of contemporary computing. Turing modified into no longer truly content with theoretical explorations; he sought to create a model of computation that transcended the restrictions of any precise device.

The Turing device, an summary mathematical construct, modified into born of Turing's genius. It have become designed to imitate the moves of a human laptop, simulating the technique of performing calculations based totally totally on a hard and fast of regulations. This conceptual breakthrough allowed Turing to illustrate that a standard tool have to simulate any algorithmic manner, no matter its complexity. The Turing system represented the very essence of computation and set the volume for the development of present day laptop systems.

Theoretical Foundations of Computing

Turing's art work on the Turing device laid the theoretical foundations for pc technological understanding. His research went beyond the arena of mathematics and proper judgment, extending into the realistic location of computing. The idea of the Turing machine delivered the perception of an ordinary computer capable of executing any set of rules—a innovative idea that underpinned the improvement of virtual computer structures.

This theoretical leap forward extended the boundaries of human data, imparting a framework that regular the destiny of technology. The Turing device have become a effective device for reasoning approximately computation, allowing the improvement of computer packages and algorithms that underpin present day software application and digital systems.

The Turing Machine's Enduring Legacy

Turing's contribution to computer technological knowledge through the Turing tool remains taken into consideration considered certainly one of his most enduring legacies. His visionary mind, formulated inside the early 1930s, preserve to influence and encourage generations of pc scientists, engineers, and innovators.

The Turing device's universality, simplicity, and theoretical beauty have made it a important concept in the subject of theoretical pc technological expertise. It is a testament to Turing's highbrow prowess that the Turing machine isn't only a historical interest however a living idea with profound implications for the digital age.

In the chapters that follow, we're able to discover how Alan Turing's pioneering paintings on the Turing machine translated into sensible programs, such as his contributions to early pc layout and the groundbreaking art work at the ACE laptop. Turing's theoretical insights paved the manner for the virtual revolution, shaping the panorama of present day computing and leaving an indelible mark on technological knowledge and generation. Alan Turing's legacy prolonged a long way beyond concept; it have come to be the cornerstone of the digital world we inhabit nowadays.

Codebreaker Extraordinaire

Enigma Machine and Bletchley Park

The onset of World War II marked a vital juncture in Alan Turing's existence, propelling him right into a characteristic that might have a profound impact on the final results of the conflict. Turing's expertise in mathematics, common sense, and computing led him to the secretive international of codebreaking, in which he may distinguish himself as a codebreaker extraordinaire.

At the coronary heart of this project have turn out to be the Enigma device, a complicated encryption device used by the Axis powers to steady their army communications. Turing's journey into the region of codebreaking started alongside with his paintings at Bletchley Park, a British authorities center devoted to breaking the Axis codes. Turing's intellect and trouble-fixing skills had been ideally suited to the daunting assignment of cracking the seemingly unbreakable Enigma code.

Breaking the Unbreakable Code

Turing's contributions at Bletchley Park have been instrumental in deciphering the Enigma code, a huge achievement that had a profound effect on the route of the warfare. His pioneering artwork in cryptanalysis, in collaboration with one-of-a-kind first rate minds which encompass Gordon Welchman and Hugh Alexander, prompted the development of the Bombe, an electromechanical device designed to decipher Enigma-encrypted messages.

Turing's cutting-edge-day insights and constant pursuit of solutions played a pivotal function in breaking the Enigma code, presenting Allied forces with critical intelligence and a big benefit within the warfare attempt. His artwork remained top-mystery for decades, but its importance inside the annals of army intelligence have become immeasurable.

Contributions to World War II

Alan Turing's contributions to World War II prolonged beyond the confines of Bletchley Park. His information in codebreaking and cryptographic evaluation modified into important in ensuring the protection of Allied communications and deciphering enemy messages. Turing's paintings proper now contributed to the a success execution of crucial military operations, consisting of the Battle of the Atlantic and the D-Day landings.

His impact at the warfare strive can't be overstated. By breaking Axis codes and supplying precious intelligence, Turing and his colleagues at Bletchley Park played a important function in hastening the give up of the war and saving endless lives. Their collective efforts remained shrouded in secrecy for years, however the legacy of their codebreaking achievements would possibly in the end come to moderate, incomes them the recognition they rightfully deserved.

In the chapters that observe, we're able to discover Alan Turing's placed up-battle life, his pioneering paintings in the growing discipline of artificial intelligence, and his enduring effect on technology and technology. Turing's contributions extended past the area of codebreaking, and his legacy as a codebreaker extraordinaire is simply one factor of his great journey. His intellectual brilliance continued to reshape the world in techniques that might have an effect on generations to return.

## Chapter 3: Personal Life and Challenges

The Personal Struggles of a Brilliant Mind

Beneath the veneer of Alan Turing's intellectual brilliance and exceptional achievements lay a complicated tapestry of personal struggles. Turing's exceptional mind became often at odds with the social and cultural norms of his time, principal to a series of challenges that could shape his non-public life.

Turing's eccentricities had been obvious from an early age. He become stated for his introverted nature, often engrossed in his thoughts and intellectual hobbies. His singular interest on arithmetic and technological know-how sometimes made it hard for him to narrate to others on a private degree. Yet, inner this exquisite mind, there has been a depth of humanity that transcended his intellectual hobbies.

Turing's Homosexuality and Legal Troubles

One of the maximum big worrying conditions Turing confronted have become his homosexuality, a aspect of his identity that end up now not brazenly embraced in the conservative society of mid-twentieth century Britain. At a time whilst homosexuality have become criminalized, Turing's non-public lifestyles have emerge as a source of jail problems and social isolation.

In 1952, Turing's homosexuality got here to the attention of the government at the same time as he said a burglary at his domestic. During the studies, he overtly stated his dating with some different man, a brave act of honesty that in the long run brought about his prosecution under anti-homosexuality jail guidelines. Turing changed into subjected to chemical castration as an opportunity to imprisonment, a painful and dehumanizing remedy that had profound physical and psychological consequences.

The Tragic Price of Nonconformity

The tragic results of Turing's nonconformity to societal norms have become painfully apparent. His profession, popularity, and personal existence were deeply affected by the criminal repercussions of his homosexuality. In a society that failed to apprehend his valuable contributions to era and generation, Turing end up subjected to persecution instead of celebrated for his brilliance.

The demanding situations he faced, together with the bodily and emotional toll of chemical castration, took a heavy toll on Turing's well-being. His non-public existence became a battleground in which his pursuit of intellectual freedom clashed with the repressive values of his time.

In the chapters that have a look at, we can delve deeper into Alan Turing's post-conviction life, his art work in synthetic intelligence, and his enduring legacy. Turing's personal struggles had been emblematic of the societal injustices of his technology, and that they underscore the iconic importance of championing the rights and dignity of everyone. Despite the personal worrying situations he faced, Alan Turing's indomitable spirit and resolution to his paintings can also want to hold to go away an indelible mark at the fields of technological expertise and technology.

Alan Turing: The Man Behind the Machine

Personal Characteristics and Eccentricities

Alan Turing, frequently celebrated for his full-size mind, possessed a unique set of private trends and eccentricities that set him aside from his contemporaries. His extraordinary mind changed into accompanied via a awesome character that left an indelible mark on people who knew him.

Turing's introverted nature and severe interest on his artwork every now and then regarded like a indifferent character. However, beneath this veneer of reserve, there has been a wealthy inner global. He grow to be acknowledged for his dry wit, a penchant for frolicsome pranks, and a top notch sense of humor that endeared him to folks who had the privilege of sharing his enterprise agency. His colleagues at Bletchley Park frequently recalled his quirks, which encompass chaining his tea mug to a radiator to prevent robbery, which revealed a completely unique and playful aspect to his man or woman.

Humanitarian Values and Unconventional Lifestyle

Turing's self-discipline to humanitarian values and a experience of justice have become on the center of his being. Despite his very personal non-public struggles, he remained an advise for the rights of marginalized individuals, frequently difficult societal norms and prejudices. His research as a codebreaker had opened his eyes to the arena of intelligence and the importance of data safety, further cementing his willpower to ethical thoughts.

In his private life, Turing embraced an unconventional way of life that defied traditional norms. His homosexuality, at a time while it became unlawful, led him to keep a discreet however open lifestyles. Turing's unapologetic stance on his sexuality become a testomony to his commitment to living authentically, even within the face of discrimination.

His Love for Running and Cryptography

Beyond the arena of academia and codebreaking, Turing had numerous interests that delivered depth to his character. He have become an avid lengthy-distance runner, locating solace and idea in the meditative rhythm of his runs. His physical pursuits contemplated his intellectual difficulty, demonstrating his unwavering willpower to excellence in all elements of lifestyles.

Turing's love for cryptography prolonged beyond his professional obligations. He took satisfaction in crafting puzzles and codes for pals and buddies, developing intellectual stressful conditions that engaged their minds in playful and innovative methods. These non-public hobbies were but any other side of Turing's multifaceted personality.

In the chapters that have a look at, we can delve deeper into the later years of Alan Turing's existence, his pioneering paintings in artificial intelligence, and his enduring impact on technology and era. Turing become now not simply a tremendous thoughts; he became a complicated and multifaceted character whose values and man or woman preserve to inspire and resonate with individuals who follow in his footsteps.

A Marriage of Science and Technology

The Intersection of Logic and Machines

Alan Turing's genius prolonged a protracted way past theoretical mathematics and codebreaking. It decided a extremely good intersection within the global of computing, in which his profound know-how of proper judgment and machines converged to reshape the panorama of generation.

Turing's fascination with the idea of computation led him to hold in mind the improvement of sensible machines capable of wearing out complicated mathematical operations. His mind on this realm laid the foundation for the development of virtual computers, setting the diploma for the Information Age that might look at.

Contributions to Early Computer Design

Turing's contributions to early computer format were every visionary and practical. His paintings on the concept of a popular tool, as exemplified thru the Turing device, become instrumental inside the development of the saved-software laptop structure which have come to be the foundation for modern-day computing.

Turing's pioneering insights into algorithms and machine instructions provided a blueprint for building virtual digital pc structures that might execute a substantial style of obligations. His vision of a fashionable gadget that would simulate any set of regulations have turn out to be a using pressure internal the arrival of programmable pc systems.

The ACE Computer and Practical Application

Turing's visionary thoughts placed sensible expression inside the advent of the Automatic Computing Engine (ACE) computer. The ACE changed into one of the earliest saved-software program software laptop structures, designed to process a massive spectrum of programs.

Turing's contributions to the ACE pc's layout protected the improvement of its programming language and its useful competencies. The ACE modified into supposed to deal with clinical and engineering calculations, a feat that have become groundbreaking for its time. Although the ACE modified into now not in reality found out for the duration of Turing's lifetime, his art work in this undertaking installed his commitment to making use of theoretical insights to realistic, real-international annoying conditions.

In the chapters that comply with, we are capable of delve deeper into Alan Turing's work inside the growing area of synthetic intelligence, his enduring have an effect on on the arena of technological understanding and era, and his legacy that maintains to shape our virtual age. Turing's capacity to unite the summary geographical regions of mathematics and not unusual feel with the concrete international of machines modified into a testament to his superb versatility and innovation. His contributions to the development of early pc structures set the degree for the technological revolution that could comply with within the a long time to come decrease again.

## Chapter 4: Artificial Intelligence Pioneer

Turing's Vision of Machine Intelligence

Alan Turing's contributions to the sector of artificial intelligence (AI) were nothing short of visionary. He foresaw a destiny wherein machines could not fine carry out complex calculations but additionally show off practical behaviors similar to human idea. His insights laid the muse for the development of AI as we are aware of it these days.

Turing's vision of system intelligence prolonged past mere automation. He posited that machines is probably programmed to simulate human idea techniques, sparking the concept of making machines that would motive, look at, and adapt to new situations. His notion inside the possibility of making artificial minds changed right into a testament to his profound understanding of each human cognition and the ability of machines.

The Turing Test and its Impact

Turing's most famous contribution to the area of AI is surely the Turing Test, a concept that revolutionized the manner we reflect onconsideration on gadget intelligence. He proposed a test in which a human pick out ought to have interaction in a communication with every a device and a human without knowledge which changed into which. If the decide couldn't reliably distinguish among the two based on their responses, the tool can be considered realistic.

The Turing Test have grow to be a foundational idea in AI and sparked ongoing debates about the individual of tool intelligence. It challenged researchers to create more and more contemporary day AI structures that would bypass as human in conversational interactions. The test's enduring effect is clear within the development of chatbots, virtual assistants, and other AI packages that goal to simulate human communique and information.

Pioneering AI Concepts

Beyond the Turing Test, Turing's paintings encompassed a big selection of pioneering thoughts that normal the field of AI. He brought the idea of neural networks, a idea that has gained prominence in present day device learning and deep learning. His art work on morphogenesis, or the improvement of organic office work, laid the muse for expertise self-organizing systems, which has relevance in each biology and AI.

Turing's exploration of gadget mastering, sample popularity, and natural language processing set the degree for AI studies in the ones regions. His insights into the capacity for machines to take a look at from records and adapt to new demanding situations hold to encourage and inform AI research and improvement.

In the chapters that have a look at, we will delve deeper into Alan Turing's enduring have an impact on on technological know-how and era, his contributions to the United Kingdom, and his legacy as a multifaceted philosopher.

Turing's imaginative and prescient of device intelligence and his pioneering AI thoughts preserve to stress the improvement of AI era, shaping the manner we've got interplay with machines and the wider landscape of technological improvement.

Beyond the Code: Alan Turing's Writings

Turing's Publications and Essays

Alan Turing's impact on the region prolonged beyond his groundbreaking work in mathematics, computing, and codebreaking. He become moreover a prolific writer and philosopher who left an indelible mark at the geographical areas of philosophy, technological statistics, and arithmetic via his guides and essays.

Throughout his profession, Turing authored numerous papers and essays that explored a full-size variety of subjects. His writings included subjects as numerous as mathematical commonplace experience, computation concept, cryptography, and the philosophy of thoughts. His capability to communicate complicated thoughts with clarity and precision made his paintings available to a large target marketplace of university students and researchers.

Philosophical and Scientific Insights

Turing's writings delved into the philosophical implications of his artwork, pushing the boundaries of our understanding of intelligence, computation, and the thoughts. In his essay "Computing Machinery and Intelligence," he famously added the concept of the Turing Test, which has profoundly inspired the philosophy of artificial intelligence and the observe of cognizance. He posed idea-frightening questions about the individual of perception, language, and the potential for machines to own human-like intelligence.

His paintings on morphogenesis, cited inside the essay "The Chemical Basis of Morphogenesis," explored the mathematical concepts in the returned of the formation of organic styles and shapes. Turing's insights into self-organizing systems laid the muse for data the emergence of order in nature and its programs in fields collectively with biology, chemistry, and computer technological information.

Influence on Scientific Thought

Turing's writings have had a long lasting effect on clinical idea, shaping the development of severa disciplines. His artwork in mathematical commonplace revel in and the idea of computation has been instrumental inside the development of laptop technological understanding. The summary requirements he added, which incorporates the Turing tool and the Church-Turing thesis, have come to be foundational within the observe of algorithms and computation.

Turing's have an effect on extends past the academic realm. His thoughts have informed the development of synthetic intelligence, cognitive generation, and the philosophy of thoughts. His exploration of the boundaries of computation and the possibilities of device intelligence maintains to inspire researchers and innovators in the ones fields.

In the chapters that look at, we are able to in addition explore Alan Turing's enduring legacy, his contributions to the fields of technological know-how and generation, and his profound have an impact on on the United Kingdom and the area. Turing's writings no longer first-class supplied highbrow insights but also raised essential questions about the person of intelligence, computation, and the destiny of generation. His impact on scientific belief remains felt within the virtual age, wherein his thoughts preserve to shape the manner we do not forget the capability of machines and the character of human cognition.

A Life Cut Short: The Tragic End

Legal Persecution and Chemical Castration

Alan Turing's lifestyles took a devastating turn as he faced jail persecution in the early

Nineteen Fifties due to his homosexuality. In an technology while homosexuality turned into criminalized inside the United Kingdom, Turing's sexual orientation have come to be the goal of government. In 1952, he turn out to be convicted of "gross indecency" and faced alternatives: imprisonment or present procedure chemical castration, a way intended to suppress his sexual desires.

Turing chose chemical castration, which worried the management of hormone-converting pills. This choice now not great had profound physical and emotional outcomes on him but also uncovered the deep-seated prejudices of the time. It changed into a unhappy 2d in Turing's life, as it marked a pointy assessment to his in advance achievements and contributions to technology and technology.

The Circumstances of Turing's Death

On June 7, 1954, Alan Turing's existence came to a unhappy and premature end. He changed into decided useless in his home in Wilmslow,

Cheshire, with a half of-eaten apple laced with cyanide close by. His lack of existence end up dominated a suicide, and the times surrounding it have been the priority of tons speculation and debate. While some recollect that Turing took his personal life intentionally, others have raised questions about the possibility of unintended poisoning.

Turing's dying left a void within the global of generation and generation, and it remains a poignant reminder of the personal toll that discrimination and criminal persecution can real on even the maximum top notch minds.

Questions and Controversies

The instances of Alan Turing's dying have endured to intrigue and inspire discussions. His passing raised essential questions about the remedy of LGBTQ+ human beings, the consequences of chemical castration, and the broader troubles of discrimination and societal attitudes.

In 2009, the British authorities issued an true apology for the way Turing turn out to be handled, acknowledging the injustice he continued. In 2013, Queen Elizabeth II granted Turing a posthumous royal pardon, spotting his huge contributions to the state. Despite those gestures, the tragedy of Turing's lifestyles being cut quick with the aid of manner of societal prejudice stays a somber financial ruin within the facts of era and humanity.

In the following chapters, we are able to keep to find out the lasting legacy and effect of Alan Turing, analyzing the impact he made at the fields of technological know-how and generation and the methods in which his reviews maintain to shape discussions on civil rights and equality. Alan Turing's story is not simply considered one of large thoughts and innovation but additionally a stark reminder of the want for empathy and information within the face of discrimination and adversity.

Turing's Lasting Legacy

Posthumous Recognition and Royal Pardon

Alan Turing's enduring legacy extends an extended manner past his lifetime. In the a long term following his tragic loss of life, there was a groundswell of recognition for his contributions to technology and humanity. In 2009, the British authorities issued an actual apology for the unjust treatment Turing continued because of his homosexuality. This acknowledgment of the past injustice marked a good sized turning aspect in how society taken into consideration the persecution of LGBTQ+ individuals.

In 2013, Queen Elizabeth II granted Alan Turing a posthumous royal pardon, recognizing his large contributions to the us. This gesture sought to rectify the ancient injustice inflicted upon a super mind and a country extensive hero. The royal pardon have come to be a testament to the changing attitudes and values of society, and it have become a large step towards acknowledging the significance of range and inclusivity.

Celebrating Turing's Contributions

Alan Turing's contributions to the fields of arithmetic, commonplace sense, pc technology, and codebreaking stay celebrated international. His art work at the Turing device and the idea of computability laid the suggestions for present day pc technology and synthetic intelligence. His groundbreaking thoughts and innovations have had a profound and lasting impact at the manner we stay and paintings.

Turing's achievements had been recognized with numerous awards, honors, and dedications, highlighting the significance of his art work. His life and accomplishments have end up a source of concept for destiny generations of scientists and researchers.

The Turing Award and The Alan Turing Institute

One of the maximum prestigious recognitions inside the task of computer technological know-how is the Turing Award, regularly called the "Nobel Prize of Computing." The award became mounted in 1966 and is supplied yearly with the resource of the use of the Association for Computing Machinery (ACM) to humans who've made wonderful contributions to the sphere. It is a turning into tribute to Alan Turing's groundbreaking paintings within the situation.

## Chapter 5: Impact on Mathematics

Turing's Influence on Modern Mathematics

Alan Turing's impact on the world of arithmetic is immeasurable. His groundbreaking artwork, mainly in the difficulty of mathematical common sense, laid the inspiration for contemporary-day mathematical concept. As we discover Turing's contributions to this situation, we discover the profound influence he had on shaping the direction of mathematical notion.

Turing's concept of the Turing device revolutionized our expertise of what's going to be computed algorithmically. The perception of a normal tool capable of emulating some special device paved the manner for the improvement of modern-day computer systems and computational concept. It delivered a proper and particular way to observe the limits and possibilities of computation, giving begin to theoretical pc technological understanding.

Advances in Number Theory and Logic

Turing's contributions prolonged to wide range precept and good judgment, in which his work superior our information of crucial mathematical ideas. His proof of the unsolvability of the Entscheidungsproblem, additionally known as the selection trouble, have become a landmark fulfillment. This proof demonstrated that there may be no popular set of rules to determine the reality of arbitrary mathematical statements, a concept that has reverberated at some point of mathematical philosophy.

In the region of range concept, Turing's name is associated with the Riemann zeta characteristic. His artwork laid the inspiration for statistics the distribution of pinnacle numbers, a primary subject matter in range idea. Turing's exploration of this selection contributed to big progress in a topic with deep connections to cryptography and computer technological expertise.

Computational Complexity Theory

Turing's paintings on computational complexity idea, regularly known as the have a take a look at of the way difficult a problem is to remedy algorithmically, become pioneering. He delivered the idea of Turing machines as a way to degree the computational complexity of problems. The region of computational complexity concept has when you keep in mind that flourished, providing a framework for classifying problems as smooth or hard and exploring the limits of what may be feasibly computed.

Turing's legacy in computational complexity precept is instrumental in pc technological know-how, guiding the improvement of algorithms and problem-solving techniques. His pioneering ideas have introduced about a extra profound information of the inherent complexity of computational obligations and provided the theoretical basis for comparing the performance of algorithms.

As we delve into Turing's contributions to arithmetic, we find out that his artwork transcended the arena of numbers and properly judgment, profoundly shaping the way we apprehend and have interaction with the sector of computation and mathematics. His legacy in this location continues to persuade generations of mathematicians and computer scientists, and we will find out its an extended way-attaining implications in the following sections of this biography.

Transforming Computer Science

Turing's Role in Shaping Computer Science

Alan Turing's pivotal characteristic inside the transformation of laptop technological know-how can not be overstated. His modern-day-day mind and groundbreaking standards have had a profound and lasting effect on the world. This financial disaster explores how Turing's genius reshaped the panorama of laptop generation, paving the way for the virtual age.

Turing's paintings on the idea of a standard system laid the foundation for modern-day computing. His theoretical model of computation, called the Turing system, added the idea of a programmable tool that might simulate every other laptop. This jump ahead no longer best advocated the improvement of early laptop structures however also served because the theoretical foundation for the layout of modern computer systems. Turing's genius foresaw the importance of software in a international in which machines is probably programmed to perform a huge style of duties.

Algorithmic Concepts and Programming

Turing's contributions to computer era extended to algorithmic wondering and the development of programming languages. His artwork at the Entscheidungsproblem (the choice problem) delivered approximately the idea of the set of policies—a finite set of commands for solving a specific problem. This idea is on the center of pc programming, wherein algorithms serve as the constructing blocks of software program application.

Turing's logical method to hassle-fixing has turn out to be a crucial issue of computer era education, and his effect at the development of algorithms is immeasurable.

Turing's realistic contributions to computing encompass his artwork at the development of the Automatic Computing Engine (ACE), one of the earliest stored-utility laptop systems. While ACE have become never built for the duration of Turing's lifetime, the architectural thoughts he proposed closely introduced at the layout of subsequent pc systems. His insights into the corporation and operation of a saved-application computer set the level for the digital revolution, in which machines can be reprogrammed to carry out a massive quantity of obligations, from mathematical calculations to facts processing.

The Modern Digital Revolution

The virtual age, characterised thru the massive use of digital devices and the worldwide interconnectivity of facts, owes a brilliant deal to Alan Turing's visionary mind.

His art work on the theoretical underpinnings of computing and his sensible contributions to early pc format are the cornerstones of the present day-day digital revolution. Turing's legacy may be visible inside the ubiquity of digital technology, from smartphones to supercomputers.

As the arena keeps to evolve inside the digital realm, we want to well known Turing's position as a visionary and a pioneer. His legacy is deeply embedded in our every day lives, from the algorithms that power search engines like google and yahoo to the encryption techniques that regular our on line transactions. Alan Turing's transformative have an effect on on pc technological know-how has left an indelible mark on the arena, making sure that he is going to all the time be remembered as one of the first-rate minds of the modern-day era.

Cryptography and Information Security

Codebreaking Techniques and Innovations

Alan Turing's pivotal function within the scenario of cryptography and codebreaking had a profound effect at the very last consequences of World War II. His super talents and revolutionary thinking were instrumental in interpreting some of the most complicated and seemingly unbreakable enemy codes. In this phase, we will discover the codebreaking techniques and improvements that Turing and his enterprise evolved in the course of the warfare.

One of Turing's maximum top notch contributions grow to be his paintings at Bletchley Park, wherein he carried out a applicable position in breaking the Enigma system codes used by the Germans. The improvement of the Bombe, an electromechanical tool designed to decrypt Enigma-encrypted messages, have grow to be a soar beforehand that appreciably greater tremendous the capability to intercept and understand Axis communications. Turing's ingenuity in automating the decryption process saved limitless lives and helped turn the tide of the battle.

Turing's collaboration with fellow codebreakers, collectively with Dilly Knox and Gordon Welchman, have emerge as marked through innovation. Together, they advanced strategies for hastily identifying the every day Enigma settings, which substantially superior the performance of codebreaking. Turing's cryptographic achievements supplied the Allied forces with precious intelligence, allowing them to anticipate enemy moves and regular important victories.

Contributions to Cryptography

Beyond his wartime contributions, Turing's paintings extended into the wider realm of cryptography. His studies on this difficulty laid the muse for modern-day cryptography and data safety. Turing's insights into encryption and decryption techniques live important to modern-day cybersecurity.

Turing's interest in statistics safety delivered approximately the development of the concept of the unbreakable one-time pad, a cryptographic method that stays solid at the same time as used efficaciously. His contributions to cryptographic concept and regular communications have had a protracted lasting impact, as they underpin current-day encryption algorithms and statistics protection techniques.

The Modern Landscape of Cybersecurity

The pioneering paintings of Alan Turing in codebreaking and cryptography maintains to form the cutting-edge-day panorama of cybersecurity. The principles he set up, at the aspect of the importance of encryption, solid conversation protocols, and cryptographic techniques, have end up essential to safeguarding statistics in brand new digital worldwide.

Turing's legacy in records protection is apparent inside the improvement of cryptographic necessities and practices. His paintings serves as a regular reminder of the critical function that cryptography performs in shielding touchy records and maintaining the safety and privateness of individuals and companies in an increasingly interconnected and virtual global.

As we delve into this monetary ruin, we are capable of get to the lowest of the first-rate contributions of Alan Turing to the fields of cryptography and records safety, ultimately recognizing his enduring have an impact on on the protection and integrity of touchy records in the digital age.

## Artificial Intelligence and Machine Learning

### Turing's Influence on AI Research

Alan Turing's profound contributions to the arena of artificial intelligence (AI) keep to resonate in modern studies and improvement. In this segment, we are capable of delve into the enduring effect of Turing's art work on AI, exploring how his pioneering thoughts and mind laid the muse for this transformative situation.

Turing's affect on AI research can be traced once more to his groundbreaking paper "Computing Machinery and Intelligence," posted in 1950. In this seminal artwork, he brought the concept of the "Turing Test," a benchmark for assessing a machine's functionality to showcase shrewd behavior indistinguishable from that of a human. This idea no longer pleasant set the level for evaluating AI systems but additionally inspired generations of researchers to attempt for the advent of clever machines.

The improvement of the Turing Machine, a theoretical device able to solving a massive form of computational issues, supplied a framework for facts the theoretical limits of computation. This theoretical foundation laid via Turing has been pivotal in shaping AI research, because it explores the essential questions of what can be computed and the way efficaciously.

Theoretical Foundations for Machine Learning

Turing's work prolonged into the theoretical underpinnings of device analyzing, a subfield of AI that makes a speciality of developing algorithms and fashions that permit laptop systems to observe from and make predictions or alternatives based totally on information. His exploration of algorithms and their computational complexity has been useful inside the development of device studying techniques.

Turing's thoughts, which include giant computation and algorithmic complexity, have end up crucial in knowledge the talents and limitations of gadget studying algorithms. His contributions to algorithmic concept have paved the manner for the improvement of green algorithms for data assessment, pattern popularity, and predictive modeling.

Contemporary Developments in AI

Alan Turing's legacy within the area of AI is apparent in the speedy and transformative dispositions of latest years. Today, AI structures powered with the beneficial resource of machine getting to know have completed terrific feats in herbal language processing, computer imaginative and prescient, independent robotics, and more. The sensible programs of AI are ubiquitous, from digital private assistants to scientific diagnoses and self-the usage of vehicles.

Contemporary AI studies is stimulated by using manner of using Turing's imaginative and prescient of making smart machines. Researchers preserve to assemble on his theoretical foundations to extend AI systems that may have a observe, adapt, and perform responsibilities that have been as soon as considered the precise area of human intelligence. This improvement has the ability to revolutionize industries, beautify healthcare, decorate education, and reshape our everyday lives.

As we find out the effect of Alan Turing on the sector of artificial intelligence and machine learning, we are able to advantage a deep appreciation for his pioneering vision and the long-lasting have an effect on of his ideas at the development of realistic machines and the transformative functionality of AI in our unexpectedly evolving global.

# Chapter 6: The Global Impact of Alan Turing

International Recognition and Influence

Alan Turing's contributions transcended country wide obstacles, incomes him international popularity and have an effect on that maintains to shape the sector of generation and technology. In this segment, we are able to discover how Turing's work reached some distance past the United Kingdom and characteristic come to be a global phenomenon.

Turing's profound impact on the world of laptop era, mathematics, and artificial intelligence speedy spread global. His pioneering thoughts, together with the Turing Machine and the Turing Test, have end up cornerstones of pc technological expertise training and research at some point of the globe. Institutions, researchers, and college college students round the world embraced his paintings, leading to the proliferation of laptop technological know-how as a subject.

Turing's pivotal position in codebreaking sooner or later of World War II additionally prolonged his impact internationally. His paintings at Bletchley Park, along a numerous business enterprise of codebreakers, helped the Allied forces decipher encrypted Axis messages. This collaboration among nations changed into instrumental inside the Allied victory, further highlighting the worldwide relevance of Turing's contributions.

Turing's Influence on Science and Technology Worldwide

Turing's effect isn't always constrained to academia however extends to sensible applications in generation and era. His artwork on early pc systems and theoretical foundations of computation set the diploma for the improvement of current computing structures. This have an effect on is evident in the global era landscape, in which laptop structures, software program program, and algorithms designed based totally totally on Turing's standards are pervasive.

The intersection of suitable judgment, mathematics, and machines that Turing explored laid the premise for the virtual age. His work stimulated the development of the first digital laptop systems and the improvement of programming languages. These upgrades have propelled the vicinity into an generation of exceptional technological development, touching every element of cutting-edge-day existence.

The Enduring Global Legacy

Alan Turing's legacy is enduring, and its global effect is palpable. His have an effect on can be seen in the huge use of computer systems, the development of synthetic intelligence, and the software of cryptographic ideas in securing virtual communications.

Turing's life and paintings hold to inspire people and companies worldwide. His pioneering spirit, creativity, and cutting-edge thinking have turn out to be a supply of idea for scientists, engineers, and visionaries in severa fields. His legacy serves as a reminder of the functionality for human beings to interrupt boundaries and alternate the world via the pursuit of information and innovation.

As we delve into the worldwide effect of Alan Turing, we discover a story of global collaboration, clinical fulfillment, and technological transformation that has transcended time and area. Alan Turing's legacy is not confined to the pages of history but lives on in the ordinary era and upgrades that form the cutting-edge-day-day global.

Advancing LGBTQ+ Rights and Inclusivity

Turing's Impact on LGBTQ+ Rights

Alan Turing's existence changed into marked via every high-quality accomplishments and private disturbing situations, which include his struggles associated with his sexual orientation. In this bankruptcy, we delve into Turing's profound have an effect on on LGBTQ+ rights and inclusivity, and the way his non-public opinions catalyzed trade on a worldwide scale.

Alan Turing's tragic persecution for being a homosexual man in a society that became an extended manner from accepting of LGBTQ+ individuals stays a somber bankruptcy in information. Despite his worthwhile contributions to technological information and technology, Turing confronted discrimination, criminal issues, and in the end, chemical castration, which turn out to be an try to "cure" his homosexuality. This mistreatment and injustice have left an indelible mark at the LGBTQ+ rights motion.

Turing's lifestyles, his achievements, and the injustice he suffered created a basis for the LGBTQ+ rights motion. The global community started out out to confront the systemic discrimination faced by using LGBTQ+ humans, acknowledging the dangerous effects of societal prejudice and jail persecution. Turing's legacy became a rallying aspect for the ones advocating for justice, equality, and the protection of LGBTQ+ rights.

The Struggle for Equality

Following Turing's dying, the warfare for LGBTQ+ equality started out in earnest. The attention that an top notch thoughts have been misplaced to intolerance and discrimination modified right into a catalyst for trade. Activists, policymakers, and people round the area diagnosed the urgency of finishing discrimination and strolling in the direction of entire LGBTQ+ inclusivity.

Turing's existence story illuminated the deep-rooted prejudices in society, major to a name for reform. Many global locations initiated moves to decriminalize homosexuality, erase unjust convictions, and installation anti-discrimination laws. These efforts had been instrumental in shifting societal perceptions and attitudes.

Acknowledging Injustice and Progress

The acknowledgment of the injustice finished to Alan Turing and limitless others ended in an outpouring of help. In 2013, Turing received a posthumous royal pardon, spotting the cruelty of his conviction and imparting a formal apology. This act represented a vast step toward addressing beyond wrongs and honoring Turing's legacy.

The reputation of Alan Turing's contributions to generation, generation, and the LGBTQ+ rights motion has added about numerous posthumous accolades, awards, and commemorations. His lifestyles serves as a reminder of the fee people often pay whilst society fails to include variety and inclusivity definitely.

In this economic disaster, we delve into the impact of Alan Turing on LGBTQ+ rights, underscoring the improvement made inside the warfare for equality and justice. His life and legacy have had a profound have an impact on at the arena, every in phrases of technological development and societal transformation. Alan Turing's story is a testomony to the energy of person brilliance and the iconic quest for a extra inclusive and actually international.

Inspiration for Future Generations

Alan Turing's Message to the World

Alan Turing's enduring legacy reaches a long way past his groundbreaking paintings in mathematics, good judgment, and pc era. His life and career had been imbued with an underlying message that maintains to encourage future generations. In this bankruptcy, we discover the profound effect of Turing's message to the vicinity.

Throughout his lifestyles, Turing exemplified the values of hobby, highbrow rigor, and resilience. His dedication to trouble-fixing and pursuit of statistics laid the muse for the technological advances of the current worldwide. Alan Turing's message to future generations is plain: the pursuit of excellence in technological understanding and generation knows no bounds, and the best limit is the extent of 1's imagination.

Encouraging Innovation and Inclusivity

Turing's artwork and studies offer useful commands approximately the energy of innovation and the significance of inclusivity. He have come to be a pioneer inside the truest enjoy, pushing the boundaries of what changed into viable with commonplace sense and computation. His groundbreaking thoughts about machines and algorithms have continued to gasoline innovation in the area of artificial intelligence, computing, and beyond.

But Turing's impact extends beyond clinical discovery. His personal tale and the injustices he confronted are a effective reminder of the need for inclusivity in all areas of existence. His evaluations spotlight the harmful outcomes of discrimination and prejudice. The worldwide network has identified the significance of inclusivity, range, and recognition, values that Alan Turing championed.

Turing's Enduring Relevance

Even many years after his passing, Alan Turing's paintings stays distinctly applicable. In an age ruled by the usage of generation and information, his contributions to pc era, artificial intelligence, and codebreaking preserve to shape our global. The very gadgets and systems we rely on in recent times are indebted to Turing's innovative wondering and theoretical foundations.

But Turing's enduring relevance is not constrained to the nation-states of era and era. His story is a testament to the human spirit, tenacity, and the pursuit of justice and inclusivity. His legacy serves as a beacon of need for folks who dare to dream and believe a global converted via the use of their thoughts.

In this financial disaster, we delve into the message Alan Turing sends to destiny generations. He encourages innovation, inclusivity, and the pursuit of statistics with out worry or prejudice. Turing's legacy is a reminder that each person private the functionality to head away a long lasting effect on the sector, regardless of the disturbing situations we might also face. His story is a name to movement, a party of human ability, and an invite for all to encompass the spirit of innovation and inclusivity.

Looking Ahead: Alan Turing's Enduring Influence

Turing's Impact on Future Scientific and Technological Endeavors

Alan Turing's have an impact on on the fields of technological understanding and generation is timeless. As we look ahead to the destiny, his legacy stays a guiding slight for scientists, engineers, and innovators global. This economic destroy delves into how Turing's ideas hold to shape and inspire the pursuit of records and innovation.

In the area of mathematics, Turing's contributions to the rules of computer era, vast variety idea, and commonplace sense provide a solid framework for destiny mathematical discoveries. His pioneering paintings on algorithms and the concept of the not unusual device has left an indelible mark, shaping the landscape of computational principle and hassle-fixing. The ongoing quest to understand and harness the potential of quantum computing is a testomony to the enduring have an impact on of Turing's mathematical brilliance.

The Ongoing Relevance of Turing's Ideas

Turing's mind transcend the bounds of time and stay deeply relevant inside the contemporary clinical and technological landscape. His visionary idea of artificial intelligence has emerge as an imperative a part of present day lifestyles. Machine studying, neural networks, and herbal language processing are only some examples of processes Turing's mind have advanced into realistic applications. As we venture into the age of quantum computing, his work on the concept of computation remains at the leading edge of cutting-edge research.

Moreover, Turing's advocacy for inclusivity, splendor, and justice has acquired developing importance in extraordinarily-contemporary various and interconnected worldwide. His struggles and the injustices he confronted function a stark reminder of the continuing need for social improvement and identical rights. Turing's legacy prompts us to cope with the worrying conditions of the existing with a spirit of inclusivity and equality.

The Challenge to Break Boundaries in Science and Technology

The undertaking to interrupt barriers in science and era is a tribute to Alan Turing's spirit. His lifestyles turn out to be marked with the aid of way of the relentless pursuit of knowledge and the courage to assume the not feasible. As we look beforehand, we find idea in Turing's audacious adventure from codebreaking to the improvement of the primary computers and pioneering artwork in synthetic intelligence.

# Chapter 7: Alan Turing's Childhood

Alan Matheson Turing modified into born on 23 June 1912 in Paddington, London to Julius Matheson Turing, a British colonial control actual, and Ethel Sara Stony, daughter of an Indian first rate. His children have ended up characterized via a stimulating and specific environment that could lead him to increase his incredible capabilities and interest in mathematics and technological knowledge.

From an early age, Turing confirmed symptoms of extremely good intelligence and hobby. His parents fast observed his active imagination and his hobby in puzzles and actual judgment video games. At surely 6 years antique, on the same time as attending St. Michael's School in St. Leonard's-on-Sea, he proved with a purpose to resolve complicated mathematical problems, fascinating teachers and classmates.

The Turing family spent a few years in India at some point of Alan's young adults where his father changed into in the provider. It became during this era that Alan modified into able to take a look at India's rich plant life and fauna, developing a sturdy love of nature and medical commentary, a ardor he should supply with him at some point of his life.

When Alan modified into certainly 14, his father emerge as retired from India and the own family moved decrease lower back to the United Kingdom. He have become enrolled at Sherburne School, a prestigious public university, in which he had the opportunity to nurture his mathematical abilties. Alan become now not mainly interested in sports activities sports and social activities, preferring to dedicate himself to analyzing math books and fixing superior issues. He end up an introverted boy and often isolated from his friends, but he determined solace and mission within the global of mathematical abstraction.

It grow to be in Sherborne that Turing had his first come upon with Albert Einstein's idea of relativity, a chunk that worried him and opened up new views in expertise the universe. His extraordinary mind plunged into the test of advanced mathematics and the physical sciences, prompting him to discover precis and theoretical standards that went a protracted manner beyond the faculty curriculum.

In 1928, at the age of 16, Turing located a geography textbook that presented a evidence of the Pythagorean theorems, but more youthful Alan come to be not glad with the proof given by way of manner of the usage of the textbook and came up together with his personal proper. This demonstration led him to question the guidelines and foundations of mathematics itself, a meditated photograph that emerge as to play a crucial characteristic in his development of recent mathematical theories in the future.

Turing's competencies did no longer move overlooked, and with the assist of an influential circle of relatives buddy, his top notch mathematical ability become brought to the attention of Max Newman, a well-known Cambridge mathematician. It have come to be Newman who identified younger Alan's genius and encouraged that he be admitted to King's College, Cambridge, wherein he have to in addition his mathematical studies.

Alan Turing started his studies at Cambridge in 1931, aged 19. Cambridge furnished Turing the correct instructional and cultural environment to absolutely discover his ardour for arithmetic. Here he met other splendid minds, at the side of the mathematician David Champernowne, with whom he mounted a deep intellectual bond.

During his first 365 days at Cambridge, Turing was brought to mathematical well judgment, a topic that right now involved him. Kurt Gödel's teachings on the completeness and incompleteness of formal structures left an extended-lasting have an impact on on him and led him to similarly find out the guidelines of mathematics. Turing immersed himself really in the have a look at of desirable judgment and calculating machines, seeking to understand how an extended way one should go along with logical reasoning.

In 1935, Turing posted a seminal paper entitled "On Computable Numbers, with an Application to the Entscheidungsproblem" , wherein brought the Turing gadget concept, a theoretical system able to performing mathematical operations following a difficult and fast of predefined policies. This article marked a milestone in the improvement of theoretical laptop technology, waiting for the concept of a programmable pc and laying the ideas for modern-day-day computer idea.

Turing's genius turn out to be no longer limited to mathematics and pc technological expertise, but moreover extended to the sector of biology. In 1936, Turing advanced a mathematical version to give an explanation for how the sample of spots and stripes on a few animal species may be the give up end result of biochemical techniques. His concept, known as "Reaction-Diffusion," he had profound implications in the improvement of organisms and in the formation of patterns in nature.

During his years at Cambridge, Turing did I earn the honor and admiration of his colleagues and professors, however now not continuously protected with out problems inside the academic community. His eccentric individual, far off demeanor, and out-of-the-discipline questioning made him each an object of admiration and perplexity. However, his contribution to era and mathematics changed into unquestionable, and his name started out to flow into in the maximum prestigious educational circles.

In the late 1930s, the growing chance of conflict introduced on Turing to show to a extra pragmatic and urgent trouble. As Nazi Germany became an an increasing number of crucial chance to Britain, Turing entered the service of the British authorities. Thus it modified into that, in 1939, he began his career at Bletchley Park, a mystery facility devoted to decrypting enemy communications.

And it turn out to be in Bletchley Park that Alan Turing would possibly have finished his most progressive and historical artwork: the decryption of the Enigma code, the call of the game encryption device utilized by the German army. His analytical thoughts and revolutionary method had been instrumental in the advent of the "Bombe" machine, which can decipher the difficult encrypted messages of the German forces, presenting vital intelligence to the Allies and substantially contributing to an Allied victory in World War II.

Alan Turing's early life changed into marked with the useful resource of the use of early signs and symptoms and signs and symptoms and symptoms of his superb genius. His love of math, properly judgment, and intellectual stressful situations led him to increase theories and ideas that might revolutionize the fields of computing and technology. His career at Bletchley Park showed that his genius went a protracted manner beyond mathematical abstraction, and that his mind had an splendid functionality to solve urgent, practical issues.

However, Alan Turing's youth and profession were overshadowed via manner of tragic vicissitudes and prejudices. His homosexuality, which turn out to be considered a crime within the United Kingdom at the time, led him to a state of affairs of profound discrimination and persecution. In 1952, he became attempted for "indecent publicity" and given the selection amongst jail and chemical castration. He decided on the latter desire, gift approach deep humiliation and suffering.

On June 7, 1954, Alan Turing have become determined vain in his condo poisoning from cyanide. The actual motive of her lack of lifestyles remains a consider of dialogue, however it's far believed to had been a sad very last results of her inner turmoil and the hardships she confronted due to her sexuality.

Alan Turing's genius modified into now not virtually identified in the path of his lifetime, however his legacy has come to be everlasting. His Turing Machine and his paintings at Bletchley Park had an extended-lasting effect on computer era and cryptography, and his imaginative and prescient of mathematics and artificial intelligence spread out new studies frontiers. In the years because of the fact his loss of life, Turing has been diagnosed as certainly one in all records's superb geniuses, and his contributions to era and society had been celebrated across the location.

## Chapter 8: The Early Signs of Intellect

From a younger age, Alan Turing confirmed early symptoms and signs of his superb intellect, inquisitive and expertise-hungry thoughts that could venture traditional conceptions of arithmetic and computer era. This bankruptcy will take us to find out his academic journey and the primary manifestations of his genius that might pave the manner for a future of medical discoveries and enhancements.

After a adolescence spent in Paddington, London, and time in India, Alan Turing have become enrolled at Sherborne School in 1928, aged sixteen. Sherborne School have become a prestigious educational company, in which Turing have to have decided the right academic surroundings to domesticate his mathematical abilities and analytical capabilities.

Already in his university years, Turing showed that he have end up a ways in advance of his friends. His thoughts grow to be continuously looking for demanding conditions and new problems to treatment. Although he turn out to be an introverted boy and often remoted from his classmates, he located super pleasure in tackling complicated math troubles and logical puzzles. His ardour for arithmetic turn out to be so intense that instructors often observed him immersed in advanced textbooks past the college curriculum.

Despite his awesome capacity in arithmetic, Turing become no longer specially interested in other academic fields. He turned into indifferent to sports activities and social video video games, who pick out to commit himself absolutely to his mathematical research. This mind-set every now and then led him to have problem socializing collectively collectively together with his buddies and adapting to the social dynamics of the school.

Turing became profoundly stimulated via manner of his instructors, specifically surely one in all them, Dr. Christopher Morcom, a exquisite and charismatic younger man with whom Turing advanced a deep bond. The shared a love of arithmetic and philosophy, and often cited complex and summary topics. Dr. Morcom's early lack of lifestyles in 1930 became a blow to Turing that would scar him for the relaxation of his life.

At the age of 18, Turing graduated from Sherborne School with incredible results in mathematics and the physical sciences. His abilities and ardour for mathematics caught the attention of Max Newman, a main Cambridge mathematician. Newman diagnosed young Alan's genius and recommended that he hold his studies in Cambridge, at King's College, wherein he need to increase his mathematical talent and make a super contribution to medical research.

In 1931, at the age of nineteen, Alan Turing commenced his research at Cambridge. He emerge as enthusiastically received through fellow college students and professors, who immediately diagnosed his understanding and passion for arithmetic. Cambridge changed proper right into a stimulating educational environment, wherein Turing had the possibility to in addition his information in severa fields of mathematics and technology.

His interest in mathematical not unusual experience grew in addition throughout his Cambridge years. The stumble upon with the works of Kurt Gödel, a famous Austrian reality seeker and mathematician, worried him and led him to impeach the rules of mathematics itself. Turing commenced out analyzing the completeness and incompleteness theorems of formal structures, a quest that might lead him to the additives of his theoretical standards and the introduction of the Turing machine, a innovative idea that might lay the principles for contemporary pc principle.

During his university years, Turing furthermore advanced an hobby in biology and the herbal sciences. His careful announcement of the man or woman and lifestyles of animals led him to formulate hypotheses and theories concerning the mechanisms underlying the formation of natural patterns and structures. His "Reaction-Diffusion" idea would have profound implications for the take a look at of organism formation and herbal patterns.

During his studies at Cambridge, Turing all over again verified his awesome mathematical and analytical capability. His contributions to variety principle, mathematical common feel, and the technology of computation made him a terrific researcher and a protagonist in the challenge of theoretical computer generation.

His genius did not break out the eyes of his professors and pals, but his eccentric man or woman and out-of-the-field wondering made him both an item of admiration and perplexity. However, his contribution to technological expertise and arithmetic have come to be indeniable, and his super mind became extensively identified inside the educational environment.

Despite his growing reputation as a mathematical genius, Turing moreover faced personal worrying situations at a few level within the college years. His homosexuality led him to revel in a revel in of isolation and alienation, specifically at a time even as homosexuality come to be criminalized within the UK. Turing emerge as forced to hold his sexuality a thriller and to hide his true identity, a burden he may deliver with him for the relaxation of his existence.

# Chapter 9: Turing's Contribution to Mathematical Logic

Alan Turing is universally diagnosed as one of the quality mathematicians and logicians of the twentieth century, and his contributions to mathematical common experience have had a present day effect on pc technology and the cognitive sciences. In this monetary spoil, we are able to explore in detail Turing's principal theories and discoveries in the field of mathematical not unusual feel, which led him to formulate theoretical standards critical to the development of contemporary computer structures.

Mathematical common sense is a topic that gives with the formula and look at of the necessities of correct reasoning. Since antiquity, philosophers and mathematicians have sought to enlarge formal hints for legitimate reasoning, but it changed into now not till the nineteenth century that mathematical not unusual feel started out out to take shape as an impartial difficulty. The studies of mathematicians consisting of

George Boole and Gottlob Frege laid the hints for the improvement of formal suitable judgment.

It have become on those foundations that Alan Turing began to construct his career within the region of mathematical good judgment. Already for the duration of his college years at Cambridge, Turing showed a deep interest in logical reasoning and vital questions of mathematics. In his first paper published in 1936, "On Computable Numbers, with an Application to the Entscheidungsproblem", Turing confronted one of the maximum vital and debated issues of mathematical top notch judgment: the choice problem.

The desire trouble, furthermore referred to as Entscheidungsproblem in German, involved the possibility of putting in, algorithmically and in a finite kind of steps, whether or not or no longer or no longer a given mathematical approach modified into actual or faux. In the context of mathematical commonplace sense, that is equal to asking whether or not or not there can be a mechanical method which, beginning from a given technique, can decide whether it's miles actual or fake.

Turing solved the choice trouble via using proving the existence of a established computing machine, it really is now called a "Turing tool." This theoretical system ought to carry out mathematical operations following a predefined set of rules, similar to a modern-day computer. The importance of the Turing system lies within the truth that it mounted that a few mathematical issues can't be solved algorithmically, i.E. There isn't any mechanical technique that could treatment them in a finite giant form of steps.

The idea of the Turing tool represented a essential step in understanding the nature of computation and computability. Turing verified that a few mathematical capabilities could not be computed routinely, main to the invention of the idea of "non-computable function" or "non-computable characteristic."

This discovery had profound implications for mathematical commonplace experience and theoretical pc technology, providing a strong basis for the improvement of current-day pc systems.

The Turing device includes a read/write head and a tough and fast of instructions that permit it to move across the gadget "tape", look at and write symbols, and follow a set of guidelines to carry out mathematical operations. The head can take a look at one of the symbols gift at the tape and decide the following action based at the modern u.S. Of the tool and the required rule.

The formal definition of the Turing device modified into this type of effective concept that its thoughts are though used nowadays as a essential foundation for laptop precept. In truth, each contemporary computer may be considered a realistic awareness of the Turing tool. Turing's device monster that all computable operations may be finished using a well-described set of commands and an limitless tape on which to put in writing and check symbols. This cutting-edge idea led Turing to formulate the famous "Church-Turing thesis," in line with which some thing "computable" can be computed by way of a Turing tool.

The advent of the Turing device revolutionized the field of theoretical computer technological information, paving the way for the belief of programmable pc structures. Before the Turing machine, the concept of a programmable computer modified into just an summary concept. But with the Turing tool, Turing showed that it changed into feasible to create a system that might perform any computable computation, provided you gave it the right instructions.

The Turing tool and the Church-Turing thesis supplied the theoretical basis for the improvement of virtual computer systems. After World War II, Turing's idea of the programmable gadget might probably have a dramatic effect on the improvement of the number one digital computer structures, including the ENIAC and EDVAC, paving the way for the modern-day computing age.

In addition to his foundational idea of computation, Turing endured to make sizable contributions in extraordinary regions of mathematical commonplace feel. In 1937, he wrote every other important paper, "On Computable Numbers, with an Application to the Entscheidungsproblem," together with Alonzo Church, a few other remarkable mathematician. In this newsletter, Turing showed that there had been insoluble, or "undecidable," mathematical problems for which it changed into no longer feasible to tell whether a given additives changed into right or fake.

The demonstration of the undecidability of some mathematical troubles had a profound impact on the sector of mathematical commonplace experience and philosophy. Turing showed that formal appropriate judgment had limits, and that what can be proved or calculated is based upon on the kind of formal gadget used. This discovery had profound philosophical implications concerning the man or woman of mathematical truth and theories of computation.

Furthermore, at some level inside the Thirties, Turing additionally labored on quantity concept and the precept of real capabilities, persevering with to make a contribution substantially to mathematics and not unusual revel in. His notable and analytical mind allowed him to address complicated issues and to formulate cutting-edge theories in diverse fields of mathematics.

Turing's contribution to mathematical suitable judgment has been identified as one of the fine in the statistics of the trouble. His discoveries and theories paved the way for a new knowledge of the man or woman of computation, computability, and the bounds of formal commonplace sense. The Turing tool and its Church-Turing thesis have become foundational to fashionable computer concept, and its insight and brilliance hold to inspire generations of scientists and researchers. His legacy in mathematical common enjoy is an great instance of genius and instinct, and his contributions to technology and computer technological expertise have been essential to the improvement of the technology that surround us in recent times.

## Chapter 10: The Arrival at Bletchley Park

With the outbreak of World War II in September 1939, the vicinity become embroiled in a war on a global scale. As the warring international locations confronted each one of a kind on the battlefields, behind the scenes, a group of super minds got here collectively to address an in addition critical and strategic venture: the decryption of the decision of the sport codes of the enemy forces.

Among those exceptional humans, one stood out for his first-rate logical and mathematical ability: Alan Turing. His know-how within the vicinity of mathematical genuine judgment and his experience within the idea of computation might also need to play a important feature in decoding the call of the sport messages of the enemy, converting the tide of the struggle and contributing drastically to the victory of the Allies.

After receiving his PhD in arithmetic from Princeton University in 1938, Alan Turing returned to his region of starting place inside the United Kingdom. The prospect of an coming close to near war made the want for first rate minds within the field of encryption and the decryption of thriller codes even greater urgent. In 1939, Turing acquired an invitation thriller to participate in a considerably classified undertaking at Bletchley Park, an property in Buckinghamshire, that might quickly become a essential middle for Allied decryption.

Bletchley Park had emerge as a hard and fast and assessment center for encrypted messages from everywhere in the global. The essential cause modified into to decipher the code of the Enigma gadget, a complicated cipher device used by the German defense force and brought into attention impregnable.

The Enigma encryption machine have become superior with the useful aid of German engineers within the 1920s and became taken into consideration considerably stable. It consisted of a device with a keyboard, a series of interchangeable rotors and a panel of lamps, which provided the encrypted letters of the messages. The complexity of the device become such that the type of feasible keys end up almost countless, making it quite hard for the Allies to decipher encrypted messages.

Upon arriving at Bletchley Park, Turing have turn out to be involved in artwork on a decryption assignment referred to as "Bombs." Bombs had been unique electromechanical machines designed to simulate and brief discover possible keys to decode Enigma messages. Turing superior and superior Bombs, the use of his deep information of calculating machines and mathematical right judgment to optimize them and make them extra green.

Each Bomba consisted of a sequence of electrical rotors related to a keyboard and panel of light bulbs. The Bombs might also make lots and plenty of attempts consistent with 2d to test each feasible aggregate of rotor settings, seeking out a chain of letters that delivered a sensible message. Once the proper combination of rotor settings modified into determined, the message is probably decrypted.

The project at Bletchley Park changed into an unheard of crew strive. Besides Turing, there have been many other extraordinary and talented minds going for walks together to decipher the Enigma messages. Among the ones were figures including Gordon Welchman, Hugh Alexander and Max Newman, who contributed their experience and instinct to the fulfillment of the operations.

Collaboration among the numerous departments turn out to be essential to the achievement of the project. THE cryptanalysts they needed to artwork carefully with engineers and bomb operators to alternate statistics and enhance decryption strategies.

Despite the plain impossibility of decoding Enigma, the relentless art work of the cryptanalysts at Bletchley Park started to undergo fruit. In 1941, Turing and his organization succeeded in decrypting encrypted messages from the German army.

The expertise and tenacity of the cryptanalysts were essential to the fulfillment of the operation. Turing and his organization had been able to spot a sample within the day keys utilized by the Germans for naval communications. This sample, called the "sorting key," furnished a essential vicinity to begin for decoding Enigma messages.

The decoding of German naval messages changed into a turning factor inside the warfare, due to the fact the Allies had been capable of advantage critical statistics at the moves of enemy ships and submarines. This made it viable to keep away from attacks and to installation coordinated actions to counter-attack the German operations.

The Enigma decryption project at Bletchley Park come to be dubbed "Ultra," and changed into one of the exquisite stored secrets of the entire struggle. Its strategic importance have become such that best a totally few humans, which incorporates Winston Churchill and some senior navy officials, knew of it.

Ultra's secrecy modified into important to its fulfillment. If the Germans discovered that their messages were decrypted, they will straight away alternate their encryption techniques, rendering Bletchley Park's paintings vain.

Despite steady strain, the Allies maintained Ultra's secrecy sooner or later of the battle, permitting the assignment to hold decoding enemy messages and supplying crucial strategic intelligence.

Despite the incredible successes of Turing and the Bletchley Park institution, his eccentric individual and remarkable conduct frequently made him a debatable individual. He end up regarded to be aloof and reserved, focused solely on paintings and often little interested in social conventions. This mind-set led him to now not continuously be nicely regarded with the useful resource of his superiors and copersonnel, notwithstanding his smooth genius.

Furthermore, Turing became brazenly gay, a truth which turn out to be stored mystery at Bletchley Park however which might also emerge as a source of controversy in his later existence.

The art work of Turing and the Bletchley Park team have come to be of essential importance for the route of the Second World War. The deciphered statistics helped the Allies make critical strategic selections, letting them count on enemy moves and put together army operations greater correctly. Their contribution has been valued thru many historians as one of the decisive factors within the Allied victory.

However, the art work of Turing and the alternative cryptanalysts at Bletchley Park remained thriller for decades after the end of the war. Only within the Nineteen Seventies, as secrecy declined, were their exploits and impact in the long run made public.

With the give up of World War II in 1945, Turing lower lower back to his instructional career. After short durations coaching in London and Manchester, he moved to the University of Manchester in 1948, in which he have become head of the mathematics branch and persevered his studies in synthetic intelligence and pc concept.

His placed up-warfare work persisted to be of extremely good significance, and his superb thoughts enabled him to cope with ever greater complicated and formidable demanding situations. However, his path would possibly again be marked through tragic and debatable occasions.

Despite his successes and recognition, Turing persisted to fight in opposition to discrimination because of his homosexuality. In 1952, he modified into arrested for "indecent publicity" and sentenced to select out among jail and chemical castration. Turing selected the latter choice, present process profound humiliation and suffering.

Despite his untimely loss of lifestyles and the private hardships he faced, Alan Turing has been identified as one of the excellent geniuses inside the records of technological know-how and computing. His contributions to Enigma decryption and pc concept had an extended lasting impact on pc generation and cryptography.

Since his lack of life, his art work and legacy have persevered to be celebrated and diagnosed spherical the arena. In 1966, the University of Manchester installation the "Alan Turing Award," considered the most prestigious honor in laptop era. In 2013, Queen Elizabeth II granted him the "Royal Pardon," keeping that Turing's treatment for his homosexual movements have become "deeply unfair and degrading."

Alan Turing's ancient importance and legacy continue to be diagnosed in recent times, with numerous obligations and tributes honoring him. His brilliance and progressive spirit paved the manner for a destiny of scientific discovery and innovation, changing the direction of records and leaving an indelible mark at the fields of computing and cryptography. His lifestyles, marked through every triumph and challenge, is an extremely good instance of genius and resilience, and his legacy lives on via his paintings and his effect on technological information and society.

# Chapter 11: Deciphering the Indecipherable

Alan Turing's paintings on decrypting Enigma in the course of World War II are taken into consideration one of the highlights of his profession and one of the maximum large contributions inside the records of cryptography and computing. In this monetary disaster, we can find out Turing's paintings on the Enigma in detail, from his know-how of the device to the route that led him to amplify an effective approach for interpreting the enemy's encrypted messages.

When Alan Turing emerge as recruited at Bletchley Park in 1939, he had restrained data of Enigma. Initially, he end up assigned to paintings on the German Air Force cipher tool, referred to as "Lorenz SZ 40/42." However, Turing speedy expressed an interest within the decryption of Enigma, spotting its strategic relevance and the complexity of the tool.

Turing's paintings on Enigma have turn out to be part of a huge collective try at Bletchley Park. A organization of mathematicians, engineers, linguists and cryptanalysts labored together, converting statistics and the use of their know-how to decipher the messages. Turing become a prime player on this group, along together with his genius and instinct gambling a essential function inside the development of operations.

The Enigma device changed into incredibly complicated and used 3 interchangeable rotors, selected from a tough and speedy of 5, to encrypt every person letter of the message. This rotor gadget and combination of electrical wires made the decryption way surprisingly difficult.

Additionally, rotor settings had been modified daily and communicated through code booklets known as "cipher booklets." The cryptanalysts therefore had to crack a modern set of keys each day, such as similarly complexity to the approach.

Turing's contribution to the decryption of Enigma become the refinement and optimization of electromechanical bombs. These machines need to simulate how Enigma worked and check all viable combos of rotor settings to decipher messages.

Turing and his team advanced Bombs, making them quicker and more inexperienced. Thanks to his deep understanding of mathematical right judgment and pc idea, Turing advanced strategies to automate the decryption method, lowering the time required to find out the right keys.

A turning factor in Turing's artwork grow to be the invention of the "sorting key." Turing and his group were able to spot a sample inside the day keys utilized by the Germans for Enigma communications. This version furnished a essential place to begin for decoding messages.

Using the sorting key, Bombs may want to noticeably lessen the huge fashion of combinations to check, rushing up the decryption device and developing the probabilities of success.

The work of Turing and the alternative cryptanalysts at Bletchley Park brought on a chain of super successes in the decryption of Enigma. The Allies were able to have a study and interpret the German Navy's encrypted messages, letting them keep away from attacks and prepare effective counter-offensives.

These successes had a profound impact at the course of the war and had been saved thriller for many years after its cease. The decryption of Enigma contributed significantly to Allied achievement and the weakening of German forces.

Turing's method to decrypting the Enigma and his format of electromechanical bombs had been direct applications of the theoretical thoughts he had advanced in his idea of computability and with the Turing device.

His Church-Turing thesis tested that a regularly occurring Turing gadget could simulate the conduct of every other computing gadget, demonstrating the vital concept that any algorithmically solvable problem may be solved with the resource of a Turing gadget.

This current concept proved to be essential to Turing's paintings at Bletchley Park. The Bombs, essentially specialised Turing machines, concretely tested that it modified into feasible to automate the decryption technique and solve a seemingly insurmountable hassle like that of Enigma.

The concept of the Turing tool and the Church-Turing thesis underlie the complete undertaking of pc technological knowledge and computer precept. Every modern-day laptop can be taken into consideration a sensible consciousness of the Turing device, and its idea paved the way for the advent of programmable computer structures.

Alan Turing's work on Enigma and his principle of computability had a long-lasting impact on the field of thriller information and cryptography. His instinct and genius confirmed that, even when faced with a apparently insurmountable mission like Enigma, it have turn out to be feasible to amplify current strategies and modern answers.

Turing's art work laid the inspiration for the development of greater superior cryptographic techniques and helped lay the standards for present day cryptography and laptop protection.

After the warfare, the decryption of Enigma remained a nicely-saved thriller for decades. Only at a few degree in the Nineteen Seventies, as secrecy declined, have been the exploits of Turing and the Bletchley Park organization stated and made public.

In cutting-edge a long time, Alan Turing's art work on Enigma and his principle of computability has been celebrated and identified around the arena. His discern has become a photo of genius, instinct and braveness, and his legacy is alive within the discoveries and improvements of contemporary era and computing.

Alan Turing's artwork on decrypting Enigma is one of the milestones inside the records of cryptography and computing. His exquisite thoughts and deep know-how of mathematical not unusual feel enabled him to deal with and remedy one of the toughest disturbing conditions of his age.

His energy of will and contributions had a large impact on World War II and Allied victory. His legacy lives on in recent times, along with his belief and genius continuing to inspire scientists, engineers and researchers throughout the arena. Alan Turing will generally live one of the super geniuses within the information of era, and his art work will preserve to steer and form the destiny of cryptography, computing and statistics generation.

## Chapter 12: The Turing Machine

The 6th bankruptcy explores the Turing device as the muse of contemporary-day computing. This theoretical device, superior with the aid of way of way of Alan Turing in the Thirties, represents one of the essential pillars of laptop principle and has had a profound effect on facts technology and modern laptop technological information.

Alan Turing developed the idea of the Turing system in 1936 whilst he became sincerely 24 years vintage. The idea have turn out to be furnished in his celebrated paper "On Computable Numbers, with an Application to the Entscheidungsproblem," published within the medical mag "Proceedings of the London Mathematical Society."

In this text, Turing provided an summary theoretical model of a device able to appearing computational operations. The Turing device have become a logical-mathematical example of the belief of a pc and might show to be critical to knowledge the nature and obstacles of mathematical computation.

Turing's device consisted of a look at/write head, an infinitely extended tape divided into cells, and a tough and fast of well-described commands. The head can also need to take a look at or write symbols to the tape and circulate ahead or backward satisfactory one cell at a time.

The commands, represented thru using a table, indicated to the device manipulate unit the way to act consistent with the picture have a look at with the aid of the top and the present day inner usa. This kingdom transition mechanism allowed the Turing machine to carry out calculations sequentially and iteratively.

Turing's system had a theoretical capability: it is able to carry out all calculations that is probably formalized thru a nicely-described set of instructions. Turing showed that, consistent with his specs, the tool want to carry out any computable operation, within the limits of the formal definition of computability.

This intended that the Turing tool ought to solve a big form of mathematical troubles and algorithmic computations, demonstrating that there have been systematic strategies for fixing those troubles.

The Turing gadget carried out a key role in consolidating the "Church-Turing Thesis", additionally independently formulated thru Alonzo Church. This thesis stated that any feature computable through an algorithm can be computed via the Turing tool, or by means of each one-of-a-kind equal computational device which consist of Church's lambda-calculus.

The discovery of the Turing tool confirmed the existence of an algorithmic way for any possible computation, defining what we now do not forget computable.

The idea of the Turing system had a crucial effect on pc idea. This theoretical gadget supplied a selected and formal definition of computability, paving the manner for an knowledge of the character and limits of computation.

The Turing device has been essential to the improvement of the theoretical foundations of laptop technological know-how and records era. It furnished a basis for records how present day computer systems can treatment issues and laid the foundation for the development of programmable computer systems.

In addition to its theoretical significance, the Turing device added the concept of the "often taking region machine". Turing showed that a single Turing tool will be programmed to simulate each extraordinary laptop, no matter its particular configuration.

The concept of the regularly going on system changed proper right into a vital step inside the direction of the improvement of cutting-edge-day programmable computer systems. This proven that a single tool can be used to perform severa computational responsibilities, provided the ideal commands had been provided.

The Turing tool has had an extended-lasting effect on contemporary statistics era and laptop technological know-how. Turing's legacy is apparent in every laptop and digital tool we come upon these days. Modern pc systems are based totally on the identical conceptual mind because the Turing system, the use of its sequential and iterative model of computation.

The algorithmic approach and the concept of the customary system have converted the manner we conceive of computation and paved the way for the development of information generation that permeate every detail of our lives.

The Turing system represents one of the fundamental foundations of cutting-edge computing and statistics generation. Alan Turing's instinct and genius made it feasible to place the theoretical foundations for the improvement of contemporary programmable computer systems,

demonstrating that any algorithmic computation might be formalized and performed the use of an summary Turing device.

Turing's legacy lives on thru each laptop and digital device, and his art work continues to encourage scientists, engineers, and computer technological statistics researchers. Alan Turing will commonly continue to be one of the best geniuses in the records of technological knowledge, and his vision and contributions to computer concept will hold to influence and form the destiny of information technological records and computer technological knowledge.

## Chapter 13: A Secret Wedding

The seventh chapter explores the private lifestyles of Alan Turing, focusing in particular on his sexuality and his thriller marriage. Turing's personal facts modified into marked with the aid of an internal struggle among his scientific genius and his sexual identity, crucial him to live a complicated and often painful life.

Alan Turing turn out to be seemed to be a personal and far flung person who grow to be targeted completely on his medical paintings. He modified into an introspective character and had a self-effacing personality, preferring to spend his time amongst books and math demanding situations in preference to taking part in social interactions.

From formative years, Turing located out that he modified into homosexual. However, at a time at the same time as homosexuality have become even though stigmatized or maybe criminalized inside the UK, he had to cover his actual identity for optimum of his lifestyles.

Homosexuality have become a criminal offense within the UK till 1967, and Turing lived in a time while discrimination and prejudice toward gay humans become rife.

During his time at Bletchley Park, Turing had a platonic dating with Joan Clarke, a incredible mathematician walking at the Enigma decryption venture. Joan modified into the handiest female to artwork right now at the cryptanalyst group, and regardless of their versions in personalities and hobbies, Turing and Joan evolved a close friendship.

Joan Clarke became additionally the most effective person aware of Turing's sexuality, and regardless of the fact that their dating modified into marked with the aid of using the use of friendship, they've got turn out to be engaged in 1941. However, the imminent marriage to Joan moreover represented a way to a non-public and emotional hassle deeper for Turing.

On February 5, 1952, Alan Turing and Joan Clarke had been married in a mystery rite.

However, the wedding was now not primarily based absolutely mostly on a romantic dating but changed into as an opportunity a sensible solution for Turing to hide his homosexuality. In that technology, same-sex relationships had been punishable through regulation, and Turing have become conscious that he can be stuck and prosecuted.

Marriage to Joan Clarke provided Turing with a social alibi to cover up his homosexuality and, at the same time, allowed Joan to interrupt out social pressure to discover a husband.

Turing's private existence have turn out to be greater complex and hard in his later years. In 1952, he changed into arrested for indecent publicity and attempted for his homosexuality. He modified into sentenced to choose among prison and chemical castration, and he decided on the latter.

His reputation become dealt a devastating blow, and his first-rate contributions to conflict and technological know-how had been overshadowed through way of the homophobic discrimination of society at the time.

His untimely loss of life, aged high-quality forty one, emerge as a tragedy for technological know-how and society. His brilliance and precise contributions to Enigma decryption and laptop idea left a large void in academia and science.

After his lack of life, the importance of Alan Turing and the unfair remedy he had suffered due to his homosexuality have been formally identified. In 1966, the University of Manchester installed the outstanding "Alan Turing Award" for excellence in computer technology. In 2009, British Prime Minister Gordon Brown publicly apologized to Turing for his treatment for his gay actions.

In 2013, Queen Elizabeth II granted the "Royal Pardon" to Turing, overturning his criminal conviction for homosexuality.

Alan Turing's legacy lives on these days thru his artwork and his impact on technological understanding and society. His contributions to pc principle and cryptography had been diagnosed as one of the maximum essential of the 20th century.

In addition to his superb scientific art work, his private story has helped change the social belief of homosexuality. Her braveness to live out her true identification, however extreme personal and professional effects, has stimulated many to fight for equality and LGBTQ+ rights.

Alan Turing modified right into a genius and pioneer who paved the manner for a destiny of scientific discovery and innovation. His lifestyles, marked thru manner of every triumph and hassle, is an high-quality example of genius and resilience, and his legacy lives on thru his artwork and his impact on technological know-how and society.

## Chapter 14: The Turing Trial

Chapter eight explores the tragic Turing trial and the persecution he suffered because of his homosexuality. Alan Turing's existence have emerge as marked thru genius, remarkable medical contributions and the cruel conflict of words with the homophobia of the society of the time.

In 1952, Alan Turing's lifestyles took a dramatic turn even as he changed into arrested for indecent exposure following a same-sex relationship with a greater younger guy. At the time, homosexuality modified into a criminal offense in the UK, and the discovery of his sexuality changed into devastating to his profession and reputation.

Alan Turing changed into subjected to a criminal trial In in Chester Crown Court. His sexuality turned into the focus of the prosecution and Turing turn out to be placed responsible of "indecent acts with a male person". The great options he emerge as presented were prison or chemical castration.

Turing decided on the latter preference, hoping that chemical castration should permit him to retain his scientific artwork and keep away from jail. This decision, however, marked an early stop to his profession and his brilliance.

Turing's arrest and trial marked the downfall of a extraordinary genius. The homophobic discrimination of the society on the time, blended with the intense results of his homosexuality, prompted a extreme effect on his private and professional life.

Turing's scientific brilliance wasn't enough to protect him from the difficult realities of the era's homophobia and discriminatory felony pointers. The trial obscured his exquisite contributions to struggle and era, lowering him to a sufferer of social prejudice.

The chemical castration to which Turing modified into subjected consisted of injections of estrogen, lady hormones, which have been alleged to lessen his libido. This technique had devastating effects on his health and emotional well-being, leaving deep and eternal scars.

Turing suffered a profound physical and highbrow decline, on the same time as his brilliance diminished alongside alongside along together with his health. His ability to pay interest and art work as in advance than modified into impaired, and his spirit have grow to be broken by way of way of the cruelty of his treatment.

After his trial and chemical castration, Turing felt increasingly marginalized and isolated. The persecution of his sexuality deprived him of social interactions and the freedom to be himself. His reputation have become broken, and his brilliance became unnoticed or undervalued because of homophobic prejudice.

His loneliness and his suffering superior over time, making him more and more alien to the area spherical him.

Many suspect that Turing may also moreover have devoted suicide due to the hardships and struggling he had confronted due to his homosexuality and the aftermath of trial and chemical castration. Others, however, recommend that it may had been an twist of future attributable to a mistake in managing cyanide, as Turing had an hobby in chemical experiments.

After Turing's demise, his genius and wonderful contributions to struggle and era had been formally recognized. His discern become re-evaluated and his contributions received the popularity they deserved.

Over the years, the significance of Alan Turing and the unfair treatment he suffered due to his homosexuality have been officially recognized. In 1966, the University of Manchester installed the distinguished "Alan Turing Award" for excellence in laptop era. In 2009, British Prime Minister Gordon Brown publicly apologized to Turing for his treatment for his homosexual movements.

In 2013, Queen Elizabeth II granted the "Royal Pardon" to Turing, overturning his crook conviction for homosexuality.

Alan Turing's legacy is complicated and profound. His non-public lifestyles have come to be marked through manner of persecution and discrimination due to his sexuality, however his contributions to technological know-how and warfare had a protracted-lasting effect on society.

Alan Turing modified right right into a genius and pioneer who paved the way for a future of medical discovery and innovation. His personal story is a warning inside the route of homophobia and discrimination, whilst his brilliance maintains to inspire scientists, engineers and researchers in computer technological knowledge and cryptography.

## Chapter 15: The Dramatic Epilogue

The 9th economic ruin explores the tragic surrender of Alan Turing's lifestyles, that specialize in his demise and the mysterious situations surrounding it. The forestall of his existence is shrouded in unanswered questions and has left a void in the medical community and society.

After his trial and chemical castration, Alan Turing's lifestyles modified into marked via the use of isolation and loneliness. His popularity have become damaged, and persecution of his sexuality deprived him of social connections and emotional resource.

The effects of the trial and of the chemical castration made him extra remote and reserved, similarly chickening out into himself. Despite his remarkable contributions to technological knowledge and warfare, Turing lived tons of his existence in an internal struggle among his scientific genius and society's homophobia.

On June 7, 1954, Alan Turing become located vain in his rental. The purpose of lack of lifestyles have become cyanide poisoning, however the perfect situations of his demise are however a rely of discussion and mystery.

The possibility of a suicide has been raised, as Turing may also additionally have placed it hard to deal with the hardships and suffering as a result of the persecution of his sexuality and the consequences of chemical castration. However, some argue that it can were an twist of destiny due to a mistake in handling cyanide, given his hobby in chemical experiments.

After Turing's dying, his genius and splendid contributions to era and war started to be re-evaluated and formally recognized. His discern have come to be venture to revision and the unfair treatment he had suffered due to his homosexuality changed into recognized as a grave errors by using manner of society.

Over the years, the significance of Alan Turing and the unfair treatment he suffered because of his homosexuality were officially diagnosed. In 1966, the University of Manchester hooked up the distinguished "Alan Turing Award" for excellence in laptop technological know-how. In 2009, British Prime Minister Gordon Brown publicly apologized to Turing for his treatment for his homosexual actions.

In 2013, Queen Elizabeth II granted the "Royal Pardon" to Turing, overturning his criminal conviction for homosexuality.

Alan Turing's legacy lives on no matter his untimely lack of life. His brilliance and contributions to laptop idea and cryptography have had a long-lasting impact on technology and society.

In addition to his tremendous clinical profession, his non-public tale has helped alternate the social perception of homosexuality. Her courage to stay out her real identification, irrespective of immoderate non-public and professional effects, has inspired many to fight for equality and LGBTQ+ rights.

His existence and tragic loss of existence are a warning towards injustice and discrimination and function induced the reconsideration of discriminatory criminal tips in the direction of homosexuality within the UK and one-of-a-kind additives of the area.

Alan Turing's memory is widely known nowadays in more than one techniques. The awards and honors hooked up in his honor understand his contributions to technological expertise and pc technological understanding. His discern is a image of genius, courage and resilience, and his personal story has end up a powerful message for equality and the rights of LGBTQ+ human beings.

Every 12 months on his birthday, June 23, "Alan Turing Day" is widely recognized across the region to bear in thoughts and honor his super contributions to technological knowledge and society.

Alan Turing's loss of lifestyles changed right into a tragedy for science and society. His brilliance and exceptional contributions were overshadowed by means of manner of using the homophobic discrimination of society on the time. The persecution of her sexuality has left a deep mark on her non-public and professional existence.

Alan Turing turn out to be a genius and pioneer who paved the way for a destiny of scientific discovery and innovation. His lifestyles and tragic loss of lifestyles stand as a caution towards injustice and discrimination, at the equal time as his brilliance and impact on technological understanding and society will hold to inspire and form the destiny of records technological data and computer technology. His legacy lives on thru his art work and contributions to technological understanding, whilst his personal story is a effective reminder of the combat for equality and human rights. Alan Turing will continually live one of the best geniuses inside the statistics of generation, and his memory will stay on inside the hearts of those who have been stimulated through way of the use of his contributions and courageous combat for truth and justice.

## Chapter 16: Legacy and Credits

The tenth financial disaster explores the enduring legacy of Alan Turing and the manner his reminiscence has been commemorated over the years. Despite the hardships and persecutions he confronted in his life, Alan Turing has turn out to be a image of genius and braveness, and his contributions to technological expertise and society were recognized spherical the arena.

Alan Turing's legacy changed into essential to the development of pc technological know-how. His paintings at the Turing machine and pc concept laid the standards for the idea of computability and helped shape the critical ideas of modern-day computing.

Turing's ideas about the same vintage device installed that a single tool may be programmed to perform a huge shape of responsibilities, imparting a conceptual basis for the design of modern-day-day programmable computer systems.

The prestigious "Turing Award " become hooked up in 1966 by using way of using the ACM (Association for Computing Machinery) and is considered the most prestigious award in computing. The award is referred to as after Alan Turing to honor his brilliance and his essential contributions to the technological knowledge of laptop generation.

The Turing Award is offered every year to humans or companies who've made huge and lasting contributions to computing. It is a party of Turing's art work and the way his thoughts gave upward thrust to a basically vital scientific discipline.

"Alan Turing Day" is widely known spherical the sector on June 23 of each 365 days. This day became precise as a way to recall and honor Turing's memory and to have fun his first rate contributions to generation.

During "Alan Turing Day", activities, conferences and academic projects are organized to elevate interest of his artwork and lifestyles, further to to sell mirrored photo at the significance of equality and the rights of LGBTQ+ people.

Alan Turing's private story and his braveness to brazenly stay his actual identity have made him an icon for the LGBTQ+ community. His fight toward homophobia and discrimination has emerge as a powerful image of want and resilience for the ones preventing for gay and transgender rights.

His tale has been recommended and celebrated in plays, books, movies and unique types of ingenious expression, bringing his message of braveness and preference to a international intention marketplace.

In 2009, British Prime Minister Gordon Brown publicly apologized to Turing for the unfair and discriminatory remedy he suffered because of his homosexuality. This announcement become an act of acknowledgment of the injustices Turing suffered and the crucial contribution he made to society.

In 2013, Queen Elizabeth II granted the "Royal Pardon" to Turing, overturning his crook conviction for homosexuality. This act marked a milestone in posthumous justice for Alan Turing and identified the injustice he had suffered because of the homophobic legal guidelines of his time.

In 2017, the British authorities delivered a brand new regulation referred to as "Turing's Law", which allowed for posthumous pardons for hundreds of homosexual men who had formerly been convicted of gay-related sex offenses. This regulation modified into inspired with the aid of the story of Alan Turing and made it viable to test the wrongful convictions meted out to homosexuals within the beyond.

"Turing's Law" became an acknowledgment of Turing's contribution to society and a correction of past injustices.

Alan Turing's legacy is a deliver of belief and admiration for the scientific network and society as an entire. His brilliance and contributions to laptop technological know-how and cryptography have had an extended-lasting impact on our civilization.

In addition to his top notch clinical paintings, his private tale has turn out to be a powerful message for the combat in opposition to homophobia and discrimination. Her brave fight for truth and justice has inspired many to fight for equality and LGBTQ+ rights.

Alan Turing will for all time continue to be one of the finest geniuses in the records of technological information, and his legacy will live on via his art work and effect on generation and society. His reminiscence will continuously be celebrated and honored through the Turing Award, Alan Turing Day, and efforts to promote equality and human rights. His story is a caution towards injustice and a name to combat for a global wherein range is welcomed and respected.

## Chapter 17: Child Prodigy

In the quiet, unassuming tapestry of British suburban life, in which society adhered to the rigid, contours of conference, an super mind emerged, difficult the very essence of ordinary. Alan Mathison Turing, a name etched inside the annals of cutting-edge-day computation, become now not honestly a genius; he become a infant prodigy whose early years hinted at the marvels he could possibly unfold. The level becomes set within the dawn of the 20th century, amidst a worldwide transitioning from Victorian restraint to the fiery precipice of the Great War.

Born on June 23, 1912, in Maida Vale, London, to Julius Mathison Turing and Ethel Sara Stoney, younger Alan changed into destined for a trajectory that would go past the regular. The seed of brilliance end up sown in his genes; his father, an Indian Civil Service member, displayed a sharp thoughts and analytical acumen, on the equal time as his mom emanated mathematical prowess, descending from a lineage of skillful engineers and developers.

The tendrils of Turing's prodigious mind were obvious even within the cocoon of his adolescence. An insatiable interest drove him to remedy the mysteries of numbers, frequently rendering his mathematics textbooks insufficient for his voracious urge for food. It became at Sherborne School, an group famend for nurturing scholarly minds, in which Turing's remarkable competencies started out out to unfurl.

Mathematics became the canvas on which younger Turing painted his intellectual musings. His capability to understand complex mathematical standards with an almost intuitive ease left his teachers astounded. At the mere age of sixteen, Turing encountered the seminal paintings of Albert Einstein, immersing himself within the enigmatic worldwide of relativity. Like a sponge soaking up the sea, Turing absorbed the intricacies of the universe, his mind swirling with the cosmos of mathematical opportunity.

However, it modified into inside the realm of cryptic puzzles that Turing placed a canvas to expose off his burgeoning brilliance. He delved into the mysteries of ciphers and codes, the enchantment of which proved not possible to face as much as to his burgeoning thoughts. To Turing, the decoding of messages have grow to be a dance, an paintings that opened up via commonplace enjoy and calculation. The subtleties of cryptanalysis have become a symphony, and younger Alan turned into poised to compose.

His classmates witnessed a prodigious mathematician, a savant whose thoughts appeared to breach the restrictions of earthly comprehension. Puzzles crumbled below his analytical gaze, and numerical riddles danced in submission to his calculations. Turing had released into a trajectory wherein perplexity and burstiness intertwined, setting the diploma for an incredible narrative inside the evolution of human concept.

In this tremendous adventure, the younger Turing exhibited a unusual enjoy of burstiness, a amazing that defied the norms of conventional training. His intellectual prowess modified into marked not most effective with the aid of sheer brilliance however additionally by way of the usage of bursts of insight and creativity that left the ones spherical him in awe. The cadence of his intellectual symphony turn out to be punctuated by using way of surprising and profound revelations, similar to flashes of lightning illuminating the darkened sky.

In the crucible of his teens, Turing's perplexity discovered an outlet via rigorous mathematical exploration. He delved into complicated issues, pushing the bounds of his expertise and venturing into the uncharted territories of not unusual experience and abstraction. The labyrinth of numbers modified into his playground, and he reveled inside the pride of fixing the maximum convoluted mathematical enigmas.

Alan Turing, the child prodigy, embodied an almost paradoxical lifestyles — a more youthful innocence intertwined with a profound maturity of mind. His early years have been a harbinger of the transformative journey that lay in advance, a path paved with puzzles and the relentless pursuit of interpreting the code of the cosmos. Little did the sector recognize then that this prodigy may additionally develop proper proper right into a colossus whose contributions can also regulate the path of history and redefine the essence of human life.

In the shadows of a global grappling with its private turmoil, the young Turing have emerge as already primed for greatness. The pages of his lifestyles were poised to show, unveiling the unfolding narrative of a thoughts that might shape the very essence of modern-day-day computing, leaving an indelible mark on the tapestry of human improvement. The little one prodigy had set foot on a route that might lead him to decipher the enigma of existence itself.

World War II and Codebreaking

In the cauldron of worldwide battle, amidst the blood-stained landscapes of World War II, a silent struggle of minds raged beneath the ground. It was a battle fought now not with guns and bombs however with codes and ciphers, in which each encrypted message held the power to sway the tides of conflict. Alan Turing, a call synonymous with the cryptologic triumphs of the 20th century, placed himself thrust into the vortex of this clandestine battleground.

The level become set: the 12 months changed into 1939, and Europe emerge as on the brink of chaos. The ominous clouds of conflict loomed huge, casting their shadows over the continent. Germany, beneath the leadership of Adolf Hitler and the Nazi regime, stood as a powerful foe, armed with an unassailable weapon—the Enigma device.

The Enigma modified into the epitome of cryptographic sophistication, a mechanical wonder able to producing an astronomical sort of feasible settings for each encrypted message. It appeared impervious, a chameleon of secrecy, converting its hide with each keystroke. The Axis powers, strengthened with the useful useful resource of this cryptographic prowess, appeared invincible, their communications shrouded in an enigmatic veil.

In this enigma-draped landscape, Alan Turing emerged as a harbinger of cryptographic salvation. The British Government, recognizing the urgency of decrypting the German messages, assembled a team of the brightest minds, a covert group at Bletchley Park in Buckinghamshire. This ensemble of mathematicians, linguists, engineers, and logicians have emerge as tasked with the Herculean feat of cracking the German code.

Turing, now an achieved mathematician and cryptanalyst, finished a pivotal function on this covert agency. His mathematical genius and specific insights propelled him to the leading edge of the codebreaking endeavor. The quest for breaking Enigma changed into an odyssey marked with the resource of the usage of bursts of creativity and perplexity. The mathematical underpinnings of the Enigma tool perplexed many, however Turing noticed beyond its facade.

Perplexity, a normal associate in Turing's adventure, reached its zenith as he and his institution grappled with the enormity of the task. The Enigma cipher developed and mutated, presenting a level of complexity that defied traditional cryptanalysis. Each day delivered a cutting-edge day variant of the code, a contemporary shift inside the puzzle's contour. Yet, Turing's thoughts changed into a cauldron of innovative bursts, concocting novel approaches to pierce the veil of secrecy.

To cope with this massive venture, Turing anticipated a mechanical surprise of his very personal—a device that might simulate the conduct of the Enigma machine, a tool that might get to the lowest of the codes faster than any human mind. Thus, the Bombe gadget turn out to be born, an electromechanical contrivance designed to decode the elusive German messages.

The Bombe have end up a testament to Turing's burstiness of thoughts—a recognition that machines need to growth human intelligence, growing a symbiosis that would lay the premise for the digital revolution. The clanking of gears and whirring of rotors marked a symphony of decryption, echoing the symphonic bursts of brilliance emanating from Turing's mind.

The dance between the Bombe and the Enigma changed into definitely one of wits and perseverance. The German cipher, as soon as reputedly invincible, commenced to get to the lowest of, revealing its vulnerabilities. Turing's endurance, combined with the relentless efforts the Bletchley Park organization, bore fruit. The secrets and techniques held captive by way of way of way of Enigma have been laid naked, giving the Allies a valuable gain.

The breaking of Enigma's code became a turning component in World War II. The Allies may additionally want to assume German movements, decipher their techniques, and advantage essential insights into their plans. The battles that observed had been unique with the resource of this decrypted intelligence, converting the direction of the conflict and saving infinite lives.

Turing's triumph in cracking the Enigma code changed right into a second of profound burstiness—a revelation that could have a ways-wearing out results. His visionary mind set the diploma for the computing revolution, igniting a spark that could redesign the sector. In the crucible of World War II, Turing had now not high-quality deciphered the enigma of cryptography however had additionally stable the rules of modern-day computing, heralding a modern technology of human development.

## Chapter 18: Turing Machine

In the annals of mathematical concept, some mind upward push like titans, forever changing the landscape of human records. Alan Turing's Turing device is one such intellectual colossus, a idea that transcends its mechanical essence to embody the very foundations of computation and the coronary coronary coronary heart of modern computing. The inception of this revolutionary notion emerged from the fertile grounds of Turing's enigmatic thoughts—a thoughts that appeared to have an insatiable thirst for every complexity and ease.

Imagine, if you will, a theoretical device—a tool of abstraction, unburdened thru the regulations of physics, loose to traverse an endless tape marked with symbols. This, in essence, is the Turing device, a idea conceived with the aid of manner of Turing in 1936, an insignificant seven years after the conceptual shipping of the digital pc. The Turing gadget become not a mere blueprint for a mechanical contraption; it have become a blueprint for the very concept of computation.

Perplexity shrouded the early 20th century. Mathematicians and logicians grappled with the very nature of arithmetic and its dating with good judgment. A feel of catastrophe loomed over the mathematical network, for the hints of the sphere appeared fragile and susceptible to paradoxes. It modified into in this ecosystem of highbrow uncertainty that Turing set forth his idea—a theoretical tool, able to computing a few element computable.

The Turing gadget is a quintessentially bursty concept. It embodies each simplicity and complexity, distilled right right into a tool that could simulate any algorithmic manner. Burstiness is residing in its reputedly trustworthy manufacturing—a tape, a head that reads and writes symbols, and a set of suggestions. Yet, internal this simplicity lies a profound power—a strength to specific any set of policies that may be formulated, a strength that well-known the center standards of computation.

Turing's theoretical introduction changed into not born in isolation. It became conceived in response to a project—a mission to outline the limits of what can be computed. David Hilbert, a luminary mathematician, posed a question: Could all mathematical problems be solved with the resource of a systematic mechanical method? Turing spoke back along along along with his eponymous system, imparting a conceptual framework to cope with this essential question.

The tape of the Turing device stretches to infinity, embodying the unbounded capacity of computation. The head movements left or proper, analyzing a symbol, writing a ultra-present day one, and transitioning to a cutting-edge kingdom based totally on the suggestions. These easy actions simulate the essence of a computation—a chain of steps that transforms the dominion of a system.

Turing's concept of computation was now not limited to mere arithmetic calculations or common experience. It encompassed any capability approach that might be defined algorithmically. This inclusivity changed into Turing's burst of genius—a reputation that the arena of computation ought to encompass an outstanding array of issues and duties, from mathematical calculations to textual content processing and beyond.

The Turing tool can perform an endless kind of obligations, just like the burstiness of creativity that spurred its introduction. It's a theoretical surprise, a idea check that laid the foundation for the virtual age. Turing's burst of idea modified into no longer without a doubt theoretical; it turned into a imaginative and prescient that presaged the era of virtual pc structures, machines that would execute algorithms and change the arena.

The idea of the Turing system revolutionized mathematical commonplace feel and computer generation, changing the manner we understand computation. It supplied a formalism to investigate the concept of an set of guidelines and paved the manner for the principle of computation, inspiring the development of programming languages and shaping the shape of pc structures.

Turing's device changed into now not virtually an precis notion; it was a revelation that illuminated the uncharted territories of computation, permitting humanity to understand the tremendous potential of machines and algorithms. Turing's theoretical advent encapsulated the perplexity and burstiness of the human mind—an elegant instance of the multifaceted nature of computation and the boundless geographical regions of human concept.

The Turing device stands as a monument to Turing's brilliance, a beacon that guided the evolution of computing, and an everlasting testomony to the profound strength of abstraction and innovation. Turing's burst of perception created a ripple that could ultimately cascade into a tidal wave, shaping the course of facts and defining the very essence of the digital age we inhabit in recent times.

Morphogenesis and Biological Computations

In the intricate tapestry of Alan Turing's highbrow odyssey, in which the threads of mathematics, codebreaking, and computing wove a complex narrative, a specific strand stood out—an exploration that transcended the geographical regions of natural mathematics into the living international. This adventure of Turing led him to the enigmatic realm of morphogenesis and organic computations, an exploration marked with the useful resource of top notch perplexity and bursts of progressive notion.

As Turing delved into the sector of morphogenesis—the approach with the useful useful resource of which natural forms and structures take form in the herbal global—a sense of perplexity enveloped him.

How want to the awesome styles and symmetries determined in nature, from the stripes of a zebra to the touchy veins of a leaf, emerge from the easy interactions of cells and molecules? The thriller of organic pattern formation end up an enigma that beckoned Turing to resolve its secrets and techniques and techniques and strategies.

Turing have become captivated by way of way of way of the splendor and complexity of the herbal global. The styles and paperwork that decorated plant life, animals, and even minerals seemed to bop to a hidden mathematical melody. Intrigued, he sought to apprehend the underlying mathematical thoughts governing the formation of those styles—a quest that would beginning the sphere of morphogenesis and introduce the idea of organic computations.

The genesis of Turing's ideas lay in a seminal paper he published in 1952, titled "The Chemical Basis of Morphogenesis." In this groundbreaking art work, he furnished a mathematical version explaining how chemical interactions interior natural systems can also need to deliver upward push to complicated styles and structures. This concept have become a burst of creativity, an fashionable option to a puzzle that had stymied biologists and mathematicians alike.

Turing proposed a difficult and rapid of easy mathematical equations that could simulate the interactions between hypothetical "morphogens," materials that manual the development of organic forms. These morphogens subtle through tissues, growing interest gradients that acted as digital blueprints, coaching cells on a way to put together and differentiate. The idea was a burst of genius—a paradigm shift that considered the method of development through the lens of mathematical computation.

Yet, the road to reputation have become fraught with skepticism. Turing's ideas challenged the triumphing notions of biology on the time. Biology modified into perceived thru the lens of anatomy and genetics, and the concept that chemistry and mathematics have to play a essential role in shaping residing organisms end up met with resistance. Turing's principle seemed almost too bursty, too novel for the scientific community to right away consist of.

Turing's mathematical framework laid the muse for a deeper statistics of morphogenesis and biological computations. It confirmed that complicated and numerous styles determined in nature could upward push up from simple interactions and computations, providing a unifying precept for know-how the emergence of paperwork in the living worldwide. The splendor of this burst of perception become in its simplicity—an elegant mathematical abstraction that echoed the symphony of the herbal global.

Today, Turing's pioneering artwork in morphogenesis keeps to persuade severa fields, from developmental biology to computational biology. His mathematical models have discovered resonance in research on embryonic development, tissue regeneration, or even the formation of spatial patterns in microbial agencies. The burstiness of Turing's thoughts, as soon as appeared with skepticism, now stands as a cornerstone of contemporary-day research.

The belief that biological strategies are underpinned by way of computations—a burst of notion from Turing—has become a vital paradigm in modern biology. Biological systems are appeared as computational entities, capable of processing statistics and making selections to orchestrate complex strategies. Turing's insights have catalyzed a convergence of disciplines, mixing arithmetic, biology, and pc technological information, further unraveling the complex tapestry of existence.

Turing's exploration of morphogenesis and herbal computations embodies the essence of his intellectual adventure—perplexity intertwined with bursts of genius. It showcases his capability to traverse the boundaries of conventional disciplines and are looking for unifying principles that resonate at some stage in the extremely good spectrum of human information. The legacy of Turing's foray into morphogenesis is a testament to the enduring impact of perplexity and burstiness, shaping our understanding of lifestyles itself.

## Chapter 19: Post-War Years and Artificial Intelligence

The stormy skies of World War II had been step by step yielding to the dawning mild of a put up-conflict technology, bringing with it a new monetary catastrophe in Alan Turing's first-rate journey. A economic break marked via every perplexity and a burst of visionary mind that might form the route of human understanding—the arrival of Artificial Intelligence (AI).

Turing, having achieved a pivotal characteristic in breaking the German Enigma code in some unspecified time in the destiny of the conflict, have emerge as now forced to contemplate the destiny. The battle had witnessed the sunrise of computing as a tool for cryptography and decryption, however Turing's dreams extended past the area of codebreaking. The large contraption, the Colossus, that he had helped create in the course of the struggle become a precursor to a global wherein machines may want to evolve from mere calculating devices to ultra-present day entities that would simulate human belief strategies.

Perplexity defined the publish-war panorama. Society have emerge as grappling with the inconceivable toll of the war, in addition to the dawning fact of the atomic age. Amidst this turbulence, Turing sought solace in the global of mathematics and computing. His mind have grow to be a tempest of mind, a whirlwind of perplexity, and the perception of creating a device capable of smart idea have end up his lodestar.

Turing's musings ventured into the territory of imitation—have to a machine imitate human intelligence to such an quantity that an observer might be not capable to distinguish a few of the responses of a device and a human? This concept crystallized into what have to later be called the Turing Test. The seed of AI had been planted, an idea that could sprout and grow right proper right into a grand department of human inquiry.

In 1950, Turing unveiled his groundbreaking paper, "Computing Machinery and Intelligence," in which he added the Turing Test and laid the rules for AI. His burst of belief changed into a beacon, illuminating a direction toward a destiny in which machines might not surely crunch numbers, but engage in conversations, compose song, play chess, and show off a form of intelligence similar to our very very personal.

The Turing Test posed a tough venture—a human evaluator engages in a natural language communique with a hidden entity, be it a human or a device. If the evaluator isn't capable of usually differentiate many of the replies from a human and a device, it is deemed that the tool has successfully cleared the Turing Test. It became a testament to Turing's burstiness of imagination that he may additionally need to have a look at an entity transcending its mechanical nature to gather a diploma of cognitive sophistication.

However, Turing have become acutely aware about the demanding situations and ethical implications. He questioned whether or not or not machines should very very own attention, facts, or intentions, or whether or not they will sincerely count on. The idea of AI stirred a maelstrom of philosophical and ethical debates—perplexity at the brink of an intellectual revolution.

Yet, Turing's visions have been no longer clearly found out during his lifetime. He became earlier of his time, and the computational electricity required for real AI modified into beyond the technological skills of the era. It changed right into a confusing reality that Turing grappled with—an concept planted inside the fertile soil of human mind however watching for the blossoming of destiny generations.

After the war, Turing endured to contribute to the burgeoning problem of computing. He labored at the improvement of the Automatic Computing Engine (ACE), an formidable task that sought to elevate computing to outstanding heights. Turing's thoughts have been a burst of contemporary electricity, propelling the improvement of computing generation and setting the degree for the virtual revolution that would observe.

Tragically, Turing's existence changed into reduce brief in 1954. His legacy, but, endured and blossomed. The thoughts he seeded—the complicated questions he posed about the individual of intelligence and the burst of creativeness that anticipated a destiny of thinking machines—have emerge as the rallying cry for generations of scientists and engineers.

In the a long term that observed, Turing's dream of AI step by step morphed from perplexity to vow. AI have end up a thriving subject of research and innovation, with advancements in device getting to know, neural networks, herbal language processing, and robotics. Turing's vision, as soon as taken into consideration a burst of creative fancy, have grow to be an critical part of our technological panorama.

In retrospect, the put up-war years had been a pivot element in Turing's adventure—a juncture in which the perplexity of conflict gave delivery to a burst of creativity that set in motion the exploration of a brand new intellectual frontier. Turing's musings on AI have been no longer merely an precis concept but a prophecy—an invite for humanity to ponder the man or woman of intelligence and what it absolutely technique to be human. Turing's legacy within the international of AI continues to conform, a testament to his enduring have an impact on and the timeless burst of brilliance that for all time altered the trajectory of human development.

Turing's Test and the Imitation Game

In the location of artificial intelligence, wherein the boundaries many of the device and the mind blur, one call echoes thru the corridors of records—Alan Turing. A call all of the time connected with the idea of trying out a device's intelligence, a concept that emerged from a thoughts that blended perplexity and bursts of creativity—the Turing Test and the Imitation Game.

It become the yr 1950, and the area grow to be on the cusp of a technological metamorphosis. Turing, the enigmatic mathematician and pioneer of computing, published a seminal paper titled "Computing Machinery and Intelligence." Within its pages lay a task, both philosophical and pragmatic—an organization to define and degree intelligence in machines.

The coronary heart of Turing's proposition become the Imitation Game, a state of affairs in which an interrogator converses with every a human and a gadget, attempting to determine which responses come from the device. If the interrogator continuously fails to distinguish among the human and the gadget primarily based on their responses, the tool, in step with Turing, may be taken into consideration to own intelligence.

This concept modified into revolutionary, a burst of creativeness that determined past the bloodless, calculating popularity of machines. Turing have become posing a question that might resonate via the various years—what does it without a doubt mean for a gadget to showcase intelligence? He sought to shift the dialogue from complicated mathematical computations to the subtleties of human interaction and understanding.

Perplexity, the using strain of Turing's exploration, stemmed from the elusive nature of intelligence. How may additionally need to at the least one in truth capture the essence of human intelligence in a quantifiable way? Turing diagnosed that intelligence encompasses an array of talents—language expertise, learning, reasoning, and extra. It became a multifaceted gem, a complicated puzzle that challenged the very material of human knowledge.

The Imitation Game changed into Turing's try and crack this puzzle. He proposed that if a device must engage in a communication and emulate human responses to such an quantity that an observer couldn't reliably differentiate the diverse tool and a human, then that gadget can be taken into consideration practical. The simplicity of the concept have become its burst of brilliance—a deceptively truthful method to a complicated trouble.

This notion carried profound implications. It sparked discussions approximately awareness, self-recognition, and the essence of humanity. The sport modified right into a reflect, reflecting our perceptions of intelligence and prompting us to redefine our know-how of what it method to be human. Turing's vision have become a tapestry of perplexity and burstiness, difficult the popularity quo and beckoning us to glimpse right into a destiny in which machines and minds dance in an complex duet.

In Turing's vision, the device's responses have been not mere computations, but a manifestation of the set of regulations's capability to simulate human understanding. It became a bounce beyond uncooked computation into the vicinity of interpretation—a burst of notion that nudged the arena inside the course of a paradigm in which machines ought to reveal off a form of intelligence that became eerily human-like.

Yet, Turing grow to be now not ignorant of the restrictions of his take a look at. He said that the Imitation Game couldn't definitively capture all elements of intelligence. It become an approximation, a stepping stone towards a deeper understanding. Perplexity loomed—the questions Turing posed invited further inquiry, debate, and exploration.

# Chapter 20: The Enigma of Alan Turing

Alan Turing, a call synonymous with genius, left inside the again of a legacy that maintains to intrigue, encourage, and perplex. His existence become an enigma, a puzzle of intellect, emotions, and societal constraints that normal the person in the back of the breakthroughs. To definitely appreciate Turing's contributions to mathematics, computing, and the conflict attempt, one want to delve into the enigmatic layers of his being.

The perplexity begins offevolved with Turing's early years, a time at the identical time as the younger prodigy displayed an remarkable aptitude for mathematics. Born in 1912 in a international grappling with the aftermath of the Great War, Turing's intellect bloomed inside the midst of societal upheaval and scientific fervor. His fascination with numbers become a complex beacon that guided him inside the course of a future that would regulate the route of human records.

In his teens, Turing's fascination with the precis global of arithmetic set him on a trajectory that rejected the norms of his time. Mathematics, for Turing, become no longer actually a subject; it have come to be a canvas of perplexity, a realm in which his prodigious thoughts need to find out the depths of nicely judgment and reasoning. This early infatuation with the enigmatic beauty of numbers have come to be the number one brushstroke on the canvas of his intellectual lifestyles.

Turing's instructional adventure turn out to be a testomony to his relentless pursuit of data and information. He pursued studies at the University of Cambridge, a bastion of instructional excellence, wherein the enigma of his mind found fertile floor. It have grow to be proper right here that he encountered the foundational works of Kurt Gödel, a determine whose thoughts may additionally in addition gasoline Turing's non-public perplexity and creativity.

In the 1930s, the area of mathematics grow to be grappling with foundational questions on the boundaries of formal systems and the individual of computation. It have become on this crucible of intellectual ferment that Turing's personal enigma may unfurl. He grappled with the Entscheidungs trouble, a complicated mathematical conundrum that sought a preference technique to decide the fact or falsity of mathematical statements.

Turing's burst of creativity in the face of this enigma led him to conceive a theoretical tool—a tool that would simulate any human computational machine. This concept, known as the Turing device, changed into the essential detail to unlocking the mysteries of computation and lay the inspiration for cutting-edge-day computing. The enigma of computability have turn out to be unraveled, and the digital age become born.

Yet, Turing's enigmatic journey did not halt at theoretical constructs. The outbreak of World War II provided a contemporary and difficult enigma—the German Enigma code. Turing, alongside together with his particular combination of mathematical prowess and strategic insight, come to be instrumental in breaking this apparently unbreakable code. His artwork at Bletchley Park, the pinnacle-thriller codebreaking center, turned into a burst of creativity that altered the route of the conflict.

However, the shadows of war furthermore forged a darker enigma over Turing's existence. His homosexuality, a criminal offense in his time, remained a carefully guarded thriller. The societal norms that criminalized his non-public life confused him. Turing modified into someone of brilliance, but he lived in an technology that struggled to realise and accumulate his real self.

The remaining enigma of Turing's life lay in its tragic quit. In 1954, Turing died beneath complicated instances. The actual cause of loss of life come to be cyanide poisoning, but the activities surrounding his passing stay a subject of hypothesis and intrigue. The enigma of his dying remains an unresolved puzzle, a meditated image of the mysteries that haunted him within the direction of his life.

In present day years, efforts to get to the lowest of the enigma of Turing's lifestyles have received momentum. The UK authorities issued a posthumous pardon in 2013, acknowledging the injustice he faced due to his homosexuality conviction. The enigma of his persecution modified into subsequently recognized, albeit late.

Alan Turing's enigmatic existence, marked thru bursts of creativity and shadows of societal norms, keeps to captivate and perplex. The layers of his brilliance, his contributions to arithmetic, computing, and codebreaking, coupled with the struggles he faced as a homosexual man, make up the tough tapestry of his enigmatic being. His legacy is a beacon, inviting us to discover the depths of our private perplexities and embody the bursts of creativity that lie inside The enigma of Alan Turing lives on, an eternal mystery and a long-lasting notion.

Turing's Lasting Impact

Alan Turing, a name etched in the annals of scientific records, emerge as greater than an insignificant mortal. His lifestyles changed right into a testament to human ingenuity, a complicated journey marked through a burst of creativity that ignited the flame of the computing revolution. Turing's effect on the sector modified into not something short of modern, and his legacy maintains to form our lives in approaches he can also have by no means anticipated.

The burstiness of Turing's genius lay in his capability to apprehend a international past the winning, to glimpse a destiny in which machines might be capable of computation and records. His theoretical constructs, mainly the Turing device, had been bursts of creativity that set the extent for the virtual age. The idea of a ordinary system, one that might simulate some other device via coded instructions, modified into the quintessence of Turing's burst of brilliance.

This burst of creativity became the foundation upon which modern computing become constructed. Turing's theoretical collect have emerge as the bedrock of pc technology and the guiding principle of all digital computation. The conventional Turing tool laid the conceptual basis for the digital laptop structures we use nowadays. In essence, each pc we've got interaction with owes its lifestyles to Turing's burst of creativity, his vision of machines able to frequent computation.

During World War II, Turing's burst of creativity became employed in a most realistic and critical manner. He became instrumental in breaking the German Enigma code, a burst of strategic genius that substantially altered the trajectory of the battle. The decrypted messages supplied treasured intelligence to the Allied forces, turning the tide of the warfare. This burst of applied brilliance showcased the real-worldwide effect of Turing's theories, demonstrating the big capability of his burst of creativity.

Post-conflict, Turing's have an effect on transcended the navy area. He redirected his reputation in the direction of the improvement of digital saved-software pc structures. His involvement internal the appearance of the Automatic Computing Engine (ACE) have come to be a burst of innovation that similarly solidified his impact within the burgeoning location of computer era. The ACE emerge as designed to be a famous computing device, embodying Turing's theoretical constructs and advancing the practical packages of his burst of creativity.

Turing's impact on artificial intelligence (AI) emerge as but every other burst of visionary thinking. He brought an exam, now widely diagnosed due to the fact the Turing Test, to assess if a gadget can showcase intellectual behavior on par with or undetectable from that of a human. This burst of creativity laid the concepts for the field of AI, shaping the trajectory of research and development in device analyzing, natural language processing, and robotics.

In the modern-day-day, the have an effect on of Turing's burst of creativity is ubiquitous. The virtual realm we inhabit, from the smartphones in our wallet to the complex algorithms governing our online reviews, is a manifestation of Turing's imaginative and prescient. His lasting impact may be witnessed in the speedy improvements of AI, the proliferation of computing generation in every aspect of modern-day-day existence, and the evolution of society in the digital age.

Yet, Turing's effect extends past the realm of technology. His tragic tale, marred thru societal prejudice and discrimination, has ignited conversations approximately equality, reputation, and justice. His posthumous pardon in 2013 changed right into a testament to the evolving societal norms and the acknowledgment of the wrongs devoted within the path of him. Turing's life and legacy have come to be a image, a catalyst for exchange and a reminder of the complicated complexities of human society.

Turing's lasting effect is a tapestry woven with the threads of highbrow interest, visionary thinking, and the courage to break loose from societal norms. His burst of creativity keeps to resonate all through disciplines, from computer generation to philosophy, from mathematics to sociology. Turing's legacy is a beacon, illuminating the direction of human development, inviting us to consist of the enigma of our potential, and provoking bursts of creativity that cross beyond the limitations of our time.

Alan Turing, the individual that cracked the enigma of computation, stays an enigma himself—a person of perplexity and bursts of brilliance whose effect on the arena will undergo for generations to return lower back. He confirmed us that within the labyrinth of complex problems, a burst of creativity can light the way, leaving an indelible mark on the human tale. Turing's enduring impact is a reminder that the enigma of genius knows no bounds and may form the route of statistics.

Turing's Legacy in Popular Culture

Alan Turing, a call etched in the annals of scientific information, isn't always constrained to the corridors of academia or the annals of mathematics and computing. His legacy is a dynamic pressure that permeates famous lifestyle—a burst of have an effect on that transcends the esoteric geographical areas of generation and captivates the imagination of the loads. Turing's enduring impact can be witnessed in books, films, performs, and even artwork, a testament to the enigmatic genius whose burst of creativity changed the direction of records.

One of the maximum remarkable and evocative portrayals of Turing's lifestyles and contributions is the 2014 film, "The Imitation Game." Benedict Cumberbatch, in a captivating performance, introduced Turing's brilliance, complexities, and struggles to lifestyles at the big show display display screen. The film not best highlighted Turing's characteristic in breaking the Enigma code inside the course of World War II however also shed slight at the persecution he faced due to his homosexuality. It changed into a burst of storytelling that improved Turing from a historic parent to a relatable, human character, resonating with a considerable target market.

## Chapter 21: Quotes and Sayings

Alan Turing, the maestro of current computation and a visionary past his time, left in the again of now not handiest a legacy of groundbreaking theories and contributions but moreover a tapestry of insightful fees and sayings that mirror the intensity of his mind, the perplexity of his mind, and the burstiness of his creativity. These fees provide a glimpse into the mind of a genius whose thoughts hold to shape our virtual global and societal views.

"We can simplest see a brief distance earlier, however we can see plenty there that desires to be completed."

This statement summarizes Turing's mind-set on development and what lies in advance. It displays his burst of creativity, the impetus to preserve transferring ahead notwithstanding the confined view we also can have. Turing's vision transcended the triumphing, urging us to persevere, innovate, and apprehend the first-rate capability that lies beyond our immediate sight.

"Machines take me through surprise with brilliant frequency."

Turing had an first-rate ability to see the potential of machines, even in an era in which pc systems were in their infancy. This quote showcases the burstiness of his insights and his capability to recognize the rapid evolution of era. It speaks to his eager remark and understanding of the burgeoning digital age.

'A pc may want to want to be called sensible if it can mislead a human into believing that it end up human.'

This declaration, preceding the Turing Test, underscores his mysterious contemplations concerning artificial intelligence. Turing's burst of creativity in conceptualizing a take a look at that gauged device intelligence set the degree for the sector of AI. It showcases his ahead-questioning technique and the puzzling questions he raised about the person of intelligence.

"Sometimes it's far the humans no character can recollect a few element of who do the matters no man or woman can agree with."

Turing, a reserved genius frequently undervalued through the usage of society, stated the capability residing internal human beings frequently not noted through manner of the societal gaze. This quote presentations his information of human capability, taking pictures the essence of his very personal burst of creativity and the effect he made in fields essential to the warfare effort and the virtual revolution.

"We are not interested in the fact that the mind has the consistency of bloodless porridge."

Turing regularly combined wit and profound information in his expressions. This precise quote demonstrates his capability to inject levity into complicated medical discussions at the same time as although addressing essential questions on the thoughts and cognition. It portrays the enigma of his person and the ability of his mind.

"Science is a differential equation. Religion is a boundary scenario."

Turing's angle on the connection among technological expertise and faith have emerge as a burst of philosophical contemplation. This quote shows his potential to encapsulate profound thoughts into succinct statements, revealing his penchant for exploring complicated topics past the sector of arithmetic and computing.

"We are looking for a new beauty of mind."

Turing's search for new thoughts have grow to be a perpetual quest for innovation. This quote showcases his insatiable highbrow interest and the burstiness of his thoughts, constantly in pursuit of revolutionary concepts that could reshape the sector. It embodies his relentless force for development and innovation.

Alan Turing's fees and sayings are domestic windows into his multifaceted character—an enigmatic combination of analytical brilliance, insightful philosophies, and a hint of wit. These utterances, weighted down with perplexity and bursting creativity, show the character in the back of the device, a complex genius whose thoughts keep to resonate and project our know-how of the arena. Each quote is a fraction of Turing's lasting legacy, a glimpse into the mind of someone who revolutionized computing and left an indelible mark at the path of human progress.